New York Yankees 2021

A Baseball Companion

Edited by Steven Goldman and Bret Sayre

Baseball Prospectus

Craig Brown, Associate Editor
Robert Au, Harry Pavlidis and Amy Pircher, Statistics Editors

Copyright © 2021 by DIY Baseball, LLC.
All rights reserved

This book or any part thereof may not be reproduced or transmitted in any form or by any means, electronic or mechanical, including photocopying, recording, or by any information storage and retrieval system, without permission in writing from the publisher.

Limit of Liability/Disclaimer of Warranty: While the publisher and the author have used their best efforts in preparing this book, they make no representations or warranties with respect to the accuracy or completeness of the contents of this book and specifically disclaim any implied warranties of merchantability or fitness for a particular purpose. No warranty may be created or extended by sales representatives or written sales materials. The advice and strategies contained herein may not be suitable for your situation. You should consult with a professional where appropriate. Neither the publisher nor the author shall be liable for any loss of profit or any other commercial damages, including but not limited to special, incidental, consequential, or other damages.

Library of Congress Cataloging-in-Publication Data:
paperback
ISBN-13: 978-1-950716-61-6

Project Credits
Cover Design: Ginny Searle
Interior Design and Production: Amy Pircher, Robert Au
Layout: Amy Pircher, Robert Au

Baseball icon courtesy of Uberux, from https://www.shareicon.net/author/uberux

Ballpark diagram courtesy of Lou Spirito/THIRTY81 Project, https://thirty81project.com/

Manufactured in the United States of America
10 9 8 7 6 5 4 3 2 1

Table of Contents

Statistical Introduction v

Part 1: Team Analysis
Performance Graphs 3
2020 Team Performance 4
2021 Team Projections 5
Team Personnel 6
Yankee Stadium Stats 7
Yankees Team Analysis 9

Part 2: Player Analysis
Yankees Player Analysis 16
Yankees Prospects 89

Part 3: Featured Articles
Yankees All-Time Top 10 Players 103
    by Steven Goldman

A Taxonomy of 2020 Abnormalities 111
    by Rob Mains

Tranches of WAR 117
    by Russell A. Carleton

Secondhand Sport 123
    by Patrick Dubuque

Steve Dalkowski Dreaming 127
    by Steven Goldman

A Reward For A Functioning Society 131
    by Cory Frontin and Craig Goldstein

Index of Names 135

Statistical Introduction

Sports are, fundamentally, a blend of athletic endeavor and storytelling. Baseball, like any other sport, tells its stories in so many ways: in the arc of a game from the stands or a season from the box scores, in photos, or even in numbers. At Baseball Prospectus, we understand that statistics don't replace observation or any of baseball's stories, but complement everything else that makes the game so much fun.

What stats help us with is with patterns and precision, variance and value. This book can help you learn things you may not see from watching a game or hundred, whether it's the path of a career over time or the breadth of the entire MLB. We'd also never ask you to choose between our numbers and the experience of viewing a game from the cheap seats or the comfort of your home; our publication combines running the numbers with observations and wisdom from some of the brightest minds we can find. But if you *do* want to learn more about the numbers beyond what's on the backs of player jerseys, let us help explain.

Offense

We've revised our methodology for determining batting value. Long-time readers of the book will notice that we've retired True Average in favor of a new metric: Deserved Runs Created Plus (DRC+). Developed by Jonathan Judge and our stats team, this statistic measures everything a player does at the plate–reaching base, hitting for power, making outs, and moving runners over–and puts it on a scale where 100 equals league-average performance. A DRC+ of 150 is terrific, a DRC+ of 100 is average and a DRC+ of 75 means you better be an excellent defender.

DRC+ also does a better job than any of our previous metrics in taking contextual factors into account. The model adjusts for how the park affects performance, but also for things like the talent of the opposing pitcher, value of different types of batted-ball events, league, temperature and other factors. It's able to describe a player's expected offensive contribution than any other statistic we've found over the years, and also does a better job of predicting future performance as well.

The other aspect of run-scoring is baserunning, which we quantify using Baserunning Runs. BRR not only records the value of stolen bases (or getting caught in the act), but also accounts for all the stuff that doesn't show up on the back of a baseball card: a runner's ability to go first to third on a single, or advance on a fly ball.

Defense

Where offensive value is *relatively* easy to identify and understand, defensive value is ... not. Over the past dozen years, the sabermetric community has focused mostly on stats based on zone data: a real-live human person records the type of batted ball and estimated landing location, and models are created that give expected outs. From there, you can compare fielders' actual outs to those expected ones. Simple, right?

Unfortunately, zone data has two major issues. First, zone data is recorded by commercial data providers who keep the raw data private unless you pay for it. (All the statistics we build in this book and on our website use public data as inputs.) That hurts our ability to test assumptions or duplicate results. Second, over the years it has become apparent that there's quite a bit of "noise" in zone-based fielding analysis. Sometimes the conclusions drawn from zone data don't hold up to scrutiny, and sometimes the different data provided by different providers don't look anything alike, giving wildly different results. Sometimes the hard-working professional stringers or scorers might unknowingly inflict unconscious bias into the mix: for example good fielders will often be credited with more expected outs despite the data, and ballparks with high press boxes tend to score more line drives than ones with a lower press box.

Enter our Fielding Runs Above Average (FRAA). For most positions, FRAA is built from play-by-play data, which allows us to avoid the subjectivity found in many other fielding metrics. The idea is this: count how many fielding plays are made by a given player and compare that to expected plays for an average fielder at their position (based on pitcher ground ball tendencies and batter handedness). Then we adjust for park and base-out situations.

When it comes to catchers, our methodology is a little different thanks to the laundry list of responsibilities they're tasked with beyond just, well, catching and throwing the ball. By now you've probably heard about "framing" or the art of making umpires more likely to call balls outside the strike zone for strikes. To put this into one tidy number, we incorporate pitch tracking data (for the years it exists) and adjust for important factors like pitcher, umpire, batter and home-field advantage using a mixed-model approach. This grants us a number for how many strikes the catcher is personally adding to (or subtracting from) his pitchers' performance ... which we then convert to runs added or lost using linear weights.

Framing is one of the biggest parts of determining catcher value, but we also take into account blocking balls from going past, whether a scorer deems it a passed ball or a wild pitch. We use a similar approach—one that really benefits from the pitch tracking data that tells us what ends up in the dirt and what doesn't. We also include a catcher's ability to prevent stolen bases and how well they field balls in play, and *finally* we come up with our FRAA for catchers.

Pitching

Both pitching and fielding make up the half of baseball that isn't run scoring: run prevention. Separating pitching from fielding is a tough task, and most recent pitching analysis has branched off from Voros McCracken's famous (and controversial) statement, "There is little if any difference among major-league pitchers in their ability to prevent hits on balls hit in the field of play." The research of the analytic community has validated this to some extent, and there are a host of "defense-independent" pitching measures that have been developed to try and extract the effect of the defense behind a hurler from the pitcher's work.

Our solution to this quandary is Deserved Run Average (DRA), our core pitching metric. DRA seeks to evaluate a pitcher's performance, much like earned run average (ERA), the tried-and-true pitching stat you've seen on every baseball broadcast or box score from the past century, but it's very different. To start, DRA takes an event-by-event look at what the pitchers does, and adjusts the value of that event based on different environmental factors like park, batter, catcher, umpire, base-out situation, run differential, inning, defense, home field advantage, pitcher role and temperature. That mixed model gives us a pitcher's expected contribution, similar to what we do for our DRC+ model for hitters and FRAA model for catchers. (Oh, and we also consider the pitcher's effect on basestealing and on balls getting past the catcher.)

DRA is set to the scale of runs allowed per nine innings (RA9) instead of ERA, which makes DRA's scale slightly higher than ERA's. Because of this, for ease of use, we're supplying DRA-, which is much easier for the reader to parse. As with DRC+, DRA- is an "index" stat, meaning instead of using some arbitrary and shifting number to denote what's "good," average is always 100. The reason that it uses a minus rather than a plus is because like ERA, a lower number is better. Therefore a 75 DRA- describes a performance 25 percent better than average, whereas a 150 DRA- means that either a pitcher is getting extremely lucky with their results, or getting ready to try a new pitch.

Since the last time you picked up an edition of this book, we've also made a few minor changes to DRA to make it better. Recent research into "tunneling"—the act of throwing consecutive pitches that appear similar from a batter's point of view until after the swing decision point–data has given us a new contextual factor to account for in DRA: plate distance. This refers to the distance between successive pitches as they approach the plate, and while it has a smaller effect than factors like velocity or whiff rate, it still can help explain pitcher strikeout rate in our model.

Recently Added Descriptive Statistics

Returning to our 2021 edition of the book are a few figures which recently appeared. These numbers may be a little bit more familiar to those of you who have spent some time investigating baseball statistics.

Fastball Percentage

Our fastball percentage (FA%) statistic measures how frequently a pitcher throws a pitch classified as a "fastball," measured as a percentage of overall pitches thrown. We qualify three types of fastballs:

1. The traditional four-seam fastball;
2. The two-seam fastball or sinker;
3. "Hard cutters," which are pitches that have the movement profile of a cut fastball and are used as the pitcher's primary offering or in place of a more traditional fastball.

For example, a pitcher with a FA% of 67 throws any combination of these three pitches about two-thirds of the time.

Whiff Rate

Everybody loves a swing and a miss, and whiff rate (Whiff%) measures how frequently pitchers induce a swinging strike. To calculate Whiff%, we add up all the pitches thrown that ended with a swinging strike, then divide that number by a pitcher's total pitches thrown. Most often, high whiff rates correlate with high strikeout rates (and overall effective pitcher performance).

Called Strike Probability

Called Strike Probability (CSP) is a number that represents the likelihood that all of a pitcher's pitches will be called a strike while controlling for location, pitcher and batter handedness, umpire and count. Here's how it works: on each pitch, our model determines how many times (out of 100) that a similar pitch was called for a strike given those factors mentioned above, and when normalized for each batter's strike zone. Then we average the CSP for all pitches thrown by a pitcher in a season, and that gives us the yearly CSP percentage you see in the stats boxes.

As you might imagine, pitchers with a higher CSP are more likely to work in the zone, where pitchers with a lower CSP are likely locating their pitches outside the normal strike zone, for better or for worse.

Projections

Many of you aren't turning to this book just for a look at what a player has done, but for a look at what a player is going to do: the PECOTA projections. PECOTA, initially developed by Nate Silver (who has moved on to greater fame as a political analyst), consists of three parts:

1. Major-league equivalencies, which use minor-league statistics to project how a player will perform in the major leagues;
2. Baseline forecasts, which use weighted averages and regression to the mean to estimate a player's current true talent level; and
3. Aging curves, which uses the career paths of comparable players to estimate how a player's statistics are likely to change over time.

With all those important things covered, let's take a look at what's in the book this year.

Team Prospectus

Most of this book is composed of team chapters, with one for each of the 30 major-league franchises. On the first page of each chapter, you'll see a box that contains some of the key statistics for each team as well as a very inviting stadium diagram.

We start with the team name, their unadjusted 2020 win-loss record, and their divisional ranking. Beneath that are a host of other team statistics. **Pythag** presents an adjusted 2020 winning percentage, calculated by taking runs scored per game (**RS/G**) and runs allowed per game (**RA/G**) for the team, and running them through a version of Bill James' Pythagorean formula that was refined and improved by David Smyth and Brandon Heipp. (The formula is called "Pythagenpat," which is equally fun to type and to say.)

Next up is **DRC+**, described earlier, to indicate the overall hitting ability of the team either above or below league-average. Run prevention on the pitching side is covered by **DRA** (also mentioned earlier) and another metric: Fielding Independent Pitching (**FIP**), which calculates another ERA-like statistic based on strikeouts, walks, and home runs recorded. Defensive Efficiency Rating (**DER**) tells us the percentage of balls in play turned into outs for the team, and is a quick fielding shorthand that rounds out run prevention.

After that, we have several measures related to roster composition, as opposed to on-field performance. **B-Age** and **P-Age** tell us the average age of a team's batters and pitchers, respectively. **Payroll** is the combined team payroll for all on-field players, and Doug Pappas' Marginal Dollars per Marginal Win (**M$/MW**) tells us how much money a team spent to earn production above replacement level.

Next to each of these stats, we've listed each team's MLB rank in that category from first to 30th. In this, first always indicates a positive outcome and 30th a negative outcome, except in the case of salary—first is highest.

After the franchise statistics, we share a few items about the team's home ballpark. There's the aforementioned diagram of the park's dimensions (including distances to the outfield wall), a graphic showing the height of the wall from the left-field pole to the right-field pole, and a table showing three-year park factors for the stadium. The park factors are displayed as indexes where 100 is average, 110 means that the park inflates the statistic in question by 10 percent, and 90 means that the park deflates the statistic in question by 10 percent.

On the second page of each team chapter, you'll find three graphs. The first is **Payroll History** and helps you see how the team's payroll has compared to the MLB and divisional average payrolls over time. Payroll figures are current as of January 1, 2021; with so many free agents still unsigned as of this writing, the final 2021 figure will likely be significantly different for many teams. (In the meantime, you can always find the most current data at Baseball Prospectus' Cot's Baseball Contracts page.)

The second graph is **Future Commitments** and helps you see the team's future outlays, if any.

The third graph is **Farm System Ranking** and displays how the Baseball Prospectus prospect team has ranked the organization's farm system since 2007.

After the graphs, we have a **Personnel** section that lists many of the important decision-makers and upper-level field and operations staff members for the franchise, as well as any former Baseball Prospectus staff members who are currently part of the organization. (In very rare circumstances, someone might be on both lists!)

Position Players

After all that information and a thoughtful bylined essay covering each team, we present our player comments. These are also bylined, but due to frequent franchise shifts during the offseason, our bylines are more a rough guide than a perfect accounting of who wrote what.

Each player is listed with the major-league team that employed him as of early January 2021. If a player changed teams after that point via free agency, trade, or any other method, you'll be able to find them in the chapter for their previous squad.

As an example, take a look at the player comment for Padres shortstop Fernando Tatis Jr.: the stat block that accompanies his written comment is at the top of this page. First we cover biographical information (age is as of June 30, 2021) before moving onto the stats themselves. Our statistic columns include standard identifying information like **YEAR**, **TEAM**, **LVL** (level of affiliated play) and **AGE** before getting into the numbers. Next, we provide raw, untranslated

Fernando Tatis Jr. SS
Born: 01/02/99 Age: 22 Bats: R Throws: R
Height: 6'3" Weight: 217 Origin: International Free Agent, 2015

YEAR	TEAM	LVL	AGE	PA	R	2B	3B	HR	RBI	BB	K	SB	CS	AVG/OBP/SLG
2018	SA	AA	19	394	77	22	4	16	43	33	109	16	5	.286/.355/.507
2019	SD	MLB	20	372	61	13	6	22	53	30	110	16	6	.317/.379/.590
2020	SD	MLB	21	257	50	11	2	17	45	27	61	11	3	.277/.366/.571
2021 FS	SD	MLB	22	600	95	24	4	31	81	50	165	17	8	.263/.331/.499
2021 DC	SD	MLB	22	628	100	25	4	32	85	53	173	19	8	.263/.331/.499

Comparables: Darryl Strawberry, Bo Bichette, Ronald Acuña Jr.

YEAR	TEAM	LVL	AGE	PA	DRC+	BABIP	BRR	FRAA	WARP
2018	SA	AA	19	394	136	.370	3.0	SS(83): -1.9	2.4
2019	SD	MLB	20	372	118	.410	7.1	SS(83): 0.9	3.4
2020	SD	MLB	21	257	126	.306	0.7	SS(57): -5.5	0.9
2021 FS	SD	MLB	22	600	126	.318	1.7	SS -1	3.9
2021 DC	SD	MLB	22	628	126	.318	1.8	SS -1	4.0

numbers like you might find on the back of your dad's baseball cards: **PA** (plate appearances), **R** (runs), **2B** (doubles), **3B** (triples), **HR** (home runs), **RBI** (runs batted in), **BB** (walks), **K** (strikeouts), **SB** (stolen bases) and **CS** (caught stealing).

Following the basic stats is **Whiff%** (whiff rate), which denotes how often, when a batter swings, he fails to make contact with the ball. Another way to think of this number is an inverse of a hitter's contact rate.

Next, we have unadjusted "slash" statistics: **AVG** (batting average), **OBP** (on-base percentage) and **SLG** (slugging percentage). Following the slash line is **DRC+** (Deserved Runs Created Plus), which we described earlier as total offensive expected contribution compared to the league average.

BABIP (batting average on balls in play) tells us how often a ball in play fell for a hit, and can help us identify whether a batter may have been lucky or not ... but note that high BABIPs also tend to follow the great hitters of our time, as well as speedy singles hitters who put the ball on the ground.

The next item is **BRR** (Baserunning Runs), which covers all of a player's baserunning accomplishments including (but not limited to) swiped bags and failed attempts. Next is **FRAA** (Fielding Runs Above Average), which also includes the number of games previously played at each position noted in parentheses. Multi-position players have only their two most frequent positions listed here, but their total FRAA number reflects all positions played.

Our last column here is **WARP** (Wins Above Replacement Player). WARP estimates the total value of a player, which means for hitters it takes into account hitting runs above average (calculated using the DRC+ model), BRR and FRAA. Then, it makes an adjustment for positions played and gives the player a credit

New York Yankees 2021

for plate appearances based upon the difference between "replacement level"—which is derived from the quality of players added to a team's roster after the start of the season–and the league average.

The final line just below the stats box is **PECOTA** data, which is discussed further in a following section.

Catchers

Catchers are a special breed, and thus they have earned their own separate box which displays some of the defensive metrics that we've built just for them. As an example, let's check out Yasmani Grandal.

YEAR	TEAM	P. COUNT	FRM RUNS	BLK RUNS	THRW RUNS	TOT RUNS
2018	LAD	16816	15.7	0.8	0.1	16.5
2019	MIL	18740	19.4	1.8	-0.1	21.1
2020	CHW	4830	3.7	0.3	-0.2	3.8
2021	CHW	14430	16.7	-0.6	1.0	17.1
2021	CHW	14430	16.7	0.4	1.0	18.0

The **YEAR** and **TEAM** columns match what you'd find in the other stat box. **P. COUNT** indicates the number of pitches thrown while the catcher was behind the plate, including swinging strikes, fouls and balls in play. **FRM RUNS** is the total run value the catcher provided (or cost) his team by influencing the umpire to call strikes where other catchers did not. **BLK RUNS** expresses the total run value above or below average for the catcher's ability to prevent wild pitches and passed balls. **THRW RUNS** is calculated using a similar model as the previous two statistics, and it measures a catcher's ability to throw out basestealers but also to dissuade them from testing his arm in the first place. It takes into account factors like the pitcher (including his delivery and pickoff move) and baserunner (who could be as fast as Billy Hamilton or as slow as Yonder Alonso). **TOT RUNS** is the sum of all of the previous three statistics.

Pitchers

Let's give our pitchers a turn, using 2020 AL Cy Young winner Shane Bieber as our example. Take a look at his stat block: the first line and the **YEAR**, **TEAM**, **LVL** and **AGE** columns are the same as in the position player example earlier.

Here too, we have a series of columns that display raw, unadjusted statistics compiled by the pitcher over the course of a season: **W** (wins), **L** (losses), **SV** (saves), **G** (games pitched), **GS** (games started), **IP** (innings pitched), **H** (hits allowed) and **HR** (home runs allowed). Next we have two statistics that are rates: **BB/9** (walks per nine innings) and **K/9** (strikeouts per nine innings), before returning to the unadjusted K (strikeouts).

Next up is **GB%** (ground ball percentage), which is the percentage of all batted balls that were hit on the ground, including both outs and hits. Remember, this is based on observational data and subject to human error, so please approach this with a healthy dose of skepticism.

BABIP (batting average on balls in play) is calculated using the same methodology as it is for position players, but it often tells us more about a pitcher than it does a hitter. With pitchers, a high BABIP is often due to poor defense or bad luck, and can often be an indicator of potential rebound, and a low BABIP may be cause to expect performance regression. (A typical league-average BABIP is close to .290-.300.)

The metrics **WHIP** (walks plus hits per inning pitched) and **ERA** (earned run average) are old standbys: WHIP measures walks and hits allowed on a per-inning basis, while ERA measures earned runs on a nine-inning basis. Neither of these stats are translated or adjusted.

DRA- (Deserved Run Average) was described at length earlier, and measures how the pitcher "deserved" to perform compared to other pitchers. Please note that since we lack all the data points that would make for a "real" DRA for minor-league events, the DRA- displayed for minor league partial-seasons is based off of different data. (That data is a modified version of our cFIP metric, which you can find more information about on our website.)

Shane Bieber   RHP

Born: 05/31/95   Age: 26   Bats: R   Throws: R
Height: 6'3"   Weight: 200   Origin: Round 4, 2016 Draft (#122 overall)

YEAR	TEAM	LVL	AGE	W	L	SV	G	GS	IP	H	HR	BB/9	K/9	K	GB%	BABIP
2018	AKR	AA	23	3	0	0	5	5	31	26	1	0.3	8.7	30	47.3%	.278
2018	COL	AAA	23	3	1	0	8	8	48^2	30	3	1.1	8.7	47	52.0%	.227
2018	CLE	MLB	23	11	5	0	20	19	114^2	130	13	1.8	9.3	118	46.2%	.356
2019	CLE	MLB	24	15	8	0	34	33	214^1	186	31	1.7	10.9	259	44.4%	.298
2020	CLE	MLB	25	8	1	0	12	12	77^1	46	7	2.4	14.2	122	48.4%	.267
2021 FS	CLE	MLB	26	10	6	0	26	26	150	121	18	2.1	11.7	195	45.5%	.297
2021 DC	CLE	MLB	26	14	7	0	30	30	196.7	159	24	2.1	11.7	257	45.5%	.297

Comparables: Luis Severino, Danny Salazar, Joe Musgrove

YEAR	TEAM	LVL	AGE	WHIP	ERA	DRA-	WARP	MPH	FB%	WHF	CSP
2018	AKR	AA	23	0.87	1.16	61	0.9				
2018	COL	AAA	23	0.74	1.66	69	1.2				
2018	CLE	MLB	23	1.33	4.55	74	2.6	94.7	57.4%	26.2%	
2019	CLE	MLB	24	1.05	3.28	75	4.9	94.4	45.8%	30.8%	
2020	CLE	MLB	25	0.87	1.63	53	2.6	95.3	53.6%	40.7%	
2021 FS	CLE	MLB	26	1.04	2.44	64	4.4	94.7	50.0%	33.2%	44.2%
2021 DC	CLE	MLB	26	1.04	2.44	64	5.8	94.7	50.0%	33.2%	44.2%

Just like with hitters, **WARP** (Wins Above Replacement Player) is a total value metric that puts pitchers of all stripes on the same scale as position players. We use DRA as the primary input for our calculation of WARP. You might notice that relief pitchers (due to their limited innings) may have a lower WARP than you were expecting or than you might see in other WARP-like metrics. WARP does not take leverage into account, just the actions a pitcher performs and the expected value of those actions ... which ends up judging high-leverage relief pitchers differently than you might imagine given their prestige and market value.

MPH gives you the pitcher's 95th percentile velocity for the noted season, in order to give you an idea of what the *peak* fastball velocity a pitcher possesses. Since this comes from our pitch-tracking data, it is not publicly available for minor-league pitchers.

Finally, we display the three new pitching metrics we described earlier. **FB%** (fastball percentage) gives you the percentage of fastballs thrown out of all pitches. **WHF** (whiff rate) tells you the percentage of swinging strikes induced out of all pitches. **CSP** (called strike probability) expresses the likelihood of all pitches thrown to result in a called strike, after controlling for factors like handedness, umpire, pitch type, count and location.

PECOTA

All players have PECOTA projections for 2021, as well as a set of other numbers that describe the performance of comparable players according to PECOTA. All projections for 2021 are for the player at the date we went to press in early January and are projected into the league and park context as indicated by the team abbreviation. (Note that players at very low levels of the minors are too unpredictable to assess using these numbers.) All PECOTA projected statistics represent a player's projected major-league performance.

How we're doing that is a little different this season. There are really two different values that go into the final stat line that you see for PECOTA: How a player performs, and how much playing time he'll be given to perform it. In the past we've estimated playing time based on each team's roster and depth charts, and we'll continue to do that. These projections are denoted as **2021 DC**.

But in many cases, a player won't be projected for major-league playing time; most of the time this is because they aren't projected to be major-league players at all, but still developing as prospects. Or perhaps a player will provide Triple-A depth, only to have an opportunity open up because of injury. For these purposes, we're also supplying a second projection, labeled **2021 FS**, or full season. This is what we would project the player to provide in 600 plate appearances or 150 innings pitched.

Below the projections are the player's three highest-scoring comparable players as determined by PECOTA. All comparables represent a snapshot of how the listed player was performing at the same age as the current player, so if a

23-year-old pitcher is compared to Bartolo Colón, he's actually being compared to a 23-year-old Colón, not the version that pitched for the Rangers in 2018, nor to Colón's career as a whole.

A few points about pitcher projections. First, we aren't yet projecting peak velocity, so that column will be blank in the PECOTA lines. Second, projecting DRA is trickier than evaluating past performance, because it is unclear how deserving each pitcher will be of his anticipated outcomes. However, we know that another DRA-related statistic–contextual FIP or cFIP–estimates future run scoring very well. So for PECOTA, the projected DRA- figures you see are based on the past cFIPs generated by the pitcher and comparable players over time, along with the other factors described above.

If you're familiar with PECOTA, then you'll have noticed that the projection system often appears bullish on players coming off a bad year and bearish on players coming off a good year. (This is because the system weights several previous seasons, not just the most recent one.) In addition, we publish the 50th percentile projections for each player–which is smack in the middle of the range of projected production—which tends to mean PECOTA stat lines don't often have extreme results like 40 home runs or 250 strikeouts in a given season. In essence, PECOTA doesn't project very many extreme seasons.

Managers

After all those wonderful team chapters, we've got statistics for each big-league manager, all of whom are organized by alphabetical order. Here you'll find a block including an extraordinary amount of information collected from each manager's entire career. For more information on the acronyms and what they mean, please visit the Glossary at www.baseballprospectus.com.

There is one important metric that we'd like to call attention to, and you'll find it next to each manager's name: **wRM+** (weighted reliever management plus). Developed by Rob Arthur and Rian Watt, wRM+ investigates how good a manager is at using their best relievers during the moments of highest leverage, using both our proprietary DRA metric as well as Leverage Index. wRM+ is scaled to a league average of 100, and a wRM+ of 105 indicates that relievers were used approximately five percent "better" than average. On the other hand, a wRM+ of 95 would tell us the team used its relievers five percent "worse" than the average team.

While wRM+ does not have an extremely strong correlation with a manager, it is statistically significant; this means that a manager is not *entirely* responsible for a team's wRM+, but does have some effect on that number.

Part 1: Team Analysis

Performance Graphs

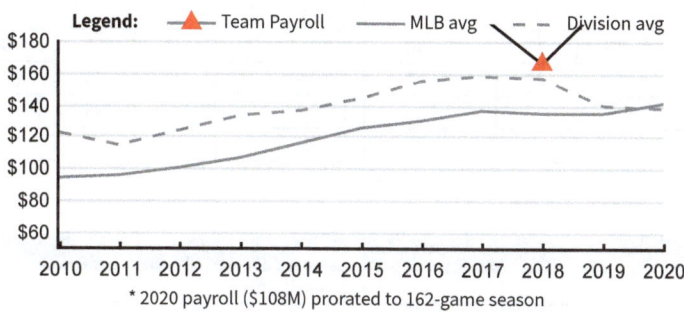

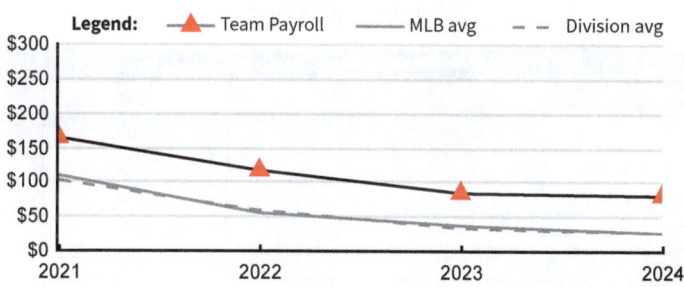

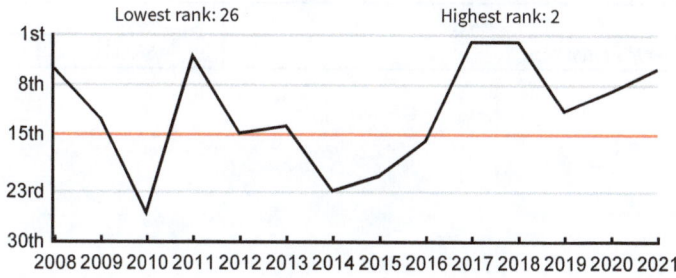

2020 Team Performance

ACTUAL STANDINGS

Team	W	L	Pct
TB	40	20	0.667
NYY	**33**	**27**	**0.550**
TOR	32	28	0.533
BAL	25	35	0.417
BOS	24	36	0.400

dWIN% STANDINGS

Team	W	L	Pct
NYY	**33**	**27**	**0.560**
TB	29	31	0.495
BOS	25	35	0.429
TOR	25	35	0.425
BAL	25	35	0.420

TOP HITTERS

Player	WARP
DJ LeMahieu	1.9
Gio Urshela	1.4
Luke Voit	1.3

TOP PITCHERS

Player	WARP
Gerrit Cole	1.5
Jordan Montgomery	0.8
Masahiro Tanaka	0.6

VITAL STATISTICS

Statistic Name	Value	Rank
Pythagenpat	.574	9th
dWin%	.560	5th
Runs Scored per Game	5.25	4th
Runs Allowed per Game	4.50	12th
Deserved Runs Created Plus	110	3rd
Deserved Run Average Minus	88	6th
Fielding Independent Pitching	4.46	14th
Defensive Efficiency Rating	.706	9th
Batter Age	29.1	28th
Pitcher Age	29.2	28th
Payroll	$108.0M	1st
Marginal $ per Marginal Win	$6.0M	24th

2021 Team Projections

PROJECTED STANDINGS

Team	W	L	Pct	+/-
NYY	**99.5**	**62.5**	**0.614**	**10**
The starting rotation was loaded with risk even before Corey Kluber and Jameson Taillon became members. At least D.J. LeMahieu should keep the lineup humming.				
TB	86.0	76.0	0.531	-22
The defending AL champions didn't really spend their winter defending anything.				
TOR	84.4	77.6	0.521	-2
They stopped a starting pitcher short of credibly claiming favorite status, but adding George Springer gives them one of the junior circuit's most lethal lineups.				
BOS	79.3	82.7	0.490	14
There's a faint flavor of their 2012-13 offseason to what Boston did this winter, and look how that year turned out.				
BAL	66.1	95.9	0.408	-1
Mike Elias was forthright about his disinterest in winning in the short term. His winter proved he was serious.				

TOP PROJECTED HITTERS

Player	WARP
Aaron Judge	4.7
DJ LeMahieu	4.6
Gleyber Torres	3.0

TOP PROJECTED PITCHERS

Player	WARP
Gerrit Cole	5.5
Corey Kluber	2.4
Jameson Taillon	1.9

FARM SYSTEM REPORT

Top Prospect	Number of Top 101 Prospects
Deivi García, #17	3

KEY DEDUCTIONS

Player	WARP
J.A. Happ	1.8
Adam Ottavino	0.6
Jonathan Holder	0.4

KEY ADDITIONS

Player	WARP
Corey Kluber	2.4
Jameson Taillon	1.9
Domingo Germán	1.3
Darren O'Day	0.8

Team Personnel

Senior Vice President, General Manager
Brian Cashman

Senior Vice President, Assistant General Manager
Jean Afterman, Esq.

Vice President, Assistant General Manager
Michael Fishman

Vice President, Baseball Operations
Tim Naehring

Manager
Aaron Boone

Yankee Stadium Stats

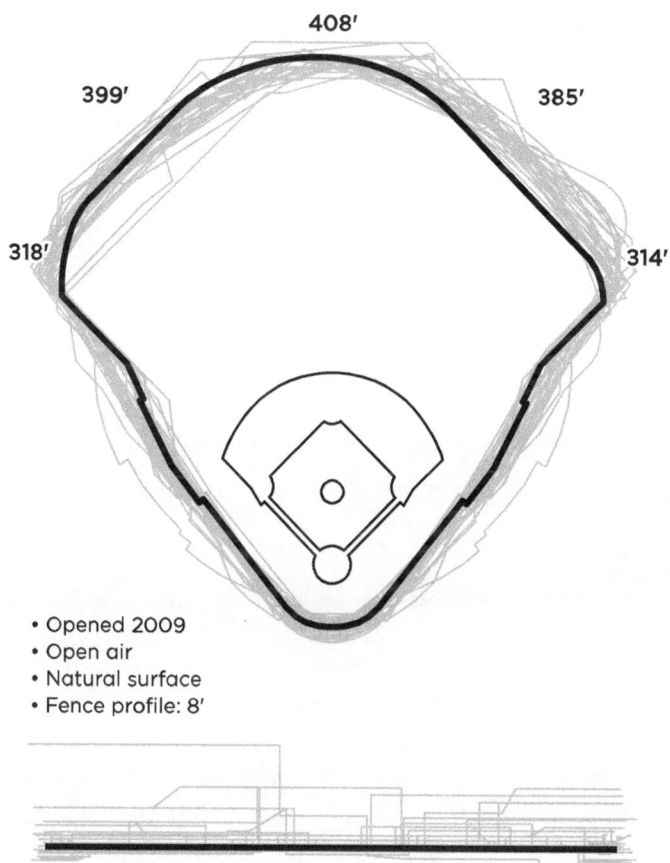

- Opened 2009
- Open air
- Natural surface
- Fence profile: 8'

Three-Year Park Factors

Runs	Runs/RH	Runs/LH	HR/RH	HR/LH
100	101	100	104	111

Yankees Team Analysis

Closer Aroldis Chapman settled into his stretch position and prepared to deliver another 3-2 pitch to his newfound nemesis, Mike Brosseau. The setting: Petco Park, Game 5 of the American League Divisional Series. Catcher Gary Sánchez implored his closer to throw a back-foot slider to the right-handed Brosseau, but Chapman shook him off. His success had always rested on his otherworldly fastball, and the arrogance that came with overpowering the opposition. That arrogance had delivered a victory to Chapman a month earlier, in his first memorable matchup with Brosseau.

For years, the Yankees and the Rays' relationship had a big brother-little brother dynamic. Dating back to the days of Jonny Gomes and Shelley Duncan, their matchups felt like the small-market Rays were trying to prove themselves to their big market foes. That dynamic changed just a month earlier. With two outs in the ninth inning of that heated contest, Chapman unleashed a ferocious 101 mph fastball that came so close to Brosseau's head that he could hear the seams on the baseball singing. Chapman won the battle that night on another high four-seamer, but he unknowingly kindled a rivalry that came to a head in Game 5 of the ALDS.

As Brosseau dug into the batter's box, preparing for the 10th pitch of his battle with Chapman, it's possible that the embers of his previous confrontation with Chapman floated through his mind. Likewise, he probably knew from experience and scouting reports that the heater was coming. He just needed it to be in the right spot. In a full count, Chapman obliged.

CRACK.

The sound of Brosseau's barrel impacting the inside fastball reverberated off Petco's empty seats so loudly that Yankees fans can still hear the echo. The only things to pierce that heartbreaking sound were the raucous cheers of the little brother winning the sibling rivalry—at least for a year. As Brosseau rounded the bases, floating on a cloud of sweet revenge, a familiar smile of shock spread across Chapman's face. That smile succinctly captures a self-imposed dilemma the Yankees face next season. It is The Smirk of Chapman™.

⚾ ⚾ ⚾

While the Brosseau home run will live on as *the* Game 5 highlight for years to come, there is a prior at-bat that captures the big-picture predicament of the Yankees. With the score tied at 1-1 in the top of the eighth inning, and Diego Castillo entering the game, Aaron Boone turned to lefty-hitting Mike Ford in place of Kyle Higashioka.

Ford was a member of the 2019 Yankees' "Next Man Up" crew. You remember them. When the Bombers suffered an unusual number of injuries throughout that season, they relied upon their 40-man roster's back-end to pull them through. After spending six years in the minors, Ford made his major-league debut when the Yankees needed him the most. He posted a 125 DRC+ while delivering critical hits along the way, including a memorable walk-off home run against Liam Hendriks that September. Unfortunately for Ford and the team, his 2020 didn't go so well. And that is putting it nicely: He lugged a slash line of .135/.226/.270 with him into the batter's box for one of the most critical at-bats of their 2020 season.

Over the last 20 years, the Yankees had the luxury of turning to their bench and calling upon accomplished veteran sluggers for moments like the one Ford found himself in. A sampling of those names includes Darryl Strawberry, Tim Raines, David Justice, Chilli Davis, Eric Chavez, Andruw Jones, Raul Ibanez, Matt Holliday and even Marcus Thames. It was always a testament to the quality, depth and versatility of the roster, but also its gaudiness; when the organization signed some new star, an older one still under contract slid down to the bench. In 2020, the Yankees' fate was resting on a player whose season should have ended when the alternate site closed shop.

To his credit, Ford battled back from 0-2 to a full count. That's when Castillo delivered a middle-middle hanging slider that Ford could only foul off. Boone had, undoubtedly, brought him into the game to crush *that* mistake. The inches between playoff glory and a missed opportunity reflect an organizational philosophy that continues to limit the full potential of the Yankees' championship-caliber core.

Title windows are a somewhat abstract construct that are nevertheless popular amongst fans and sports media. The idea is that a team's core of players have a finite amount of time together to win a championship. Title windows, then, represent a perceived expiration date that is often rooted in the exploitative nature of pre-free agency contract structures. The further away a talented group of players are from potential big paydays, the larger the window is perceived to be. This is a simplification of the concept, but you get the idea.

Professional sports are one of the few industries with an aversion to both, long-term planning and present-day investing in the product. Baseball franchises willingly think four-to-five years ahead at the most with their major-league roster, usually in an attempt to keep payrolls down and to maintain high profits. It is especially true when a particular team develops multiple prospects into productive major leaguers. Said organization is then thrust onto the clock when that happens. They've entered their title window.

This doesn't have to be the case. If we're sincere, this shouldn't be the case. It especially shouldn't be the case in an uncapped sport like baseball. Franchises should be looking beyond this arbitrary five-year window. It may be conservative to estimate that 25 out of the 30 major-league teams have the resources to extend a productive core's shelf life. This may be a naive and purist view on things, but the point of building a talented core should be to put the team in the best position to win as many titles as possible for as long as possible.

Under George Steinbrenner, the Yankees didn't concern themselves with cycles. They were the Evil Empire, almighty and immutable, a franchise that could afford to reinforce the army with as many mercenaries as necessary. It was sometimes clumsy, and almost always effective. They were the Goliath who stole away Jason Giambi, serving as the antagonists of *Moneyball* and providing the catalyst for the modern age of austerity.

Under Hal Steinbrenner, the Yankees have reimagined how they allocate their immense resources. The organization built a robust analytics department, expanded its research and development team and invested in their minor-league facilities. Brian Cashman believed the franchise was falling behind other teams implementing innovative approaches to close the competitive gap. In Cashman's mind, the team needed an internal makeover more than they required wild expenditures in the free-agent market—though both should have been in reach.

It's difficult to argue with that belief. Beyond the successful development of Aaron Judge, Gary Sánchez, Gleyber Torres and Clint Frazier in recent years (the latter two were originally acquired in trade), the front office discovered diamonds in the rough like Luke Voit and Gio Urshela. The Yankees were not only able to avoid a full teardown a few years back, but they emerged as a real championship contender. Cashman realized his vision.

The concern these days is the team appears satisfied just to have a title window. Now, they are conducting business as if the cost of a championship is greater than the reward of earning one. It is unfair to say the team is complacent: you don't spend over $300 million on Brian Cashman's White Whale, Gerrit Cole, if you're complacent; it *would* be fair to say the Yankees sit in a self-constructed purgatory. It rests between an all-out aggressive approach to maximize everything, and a satisfaction with a good but flawed roster.

Some prefer to see a financial powerhouse flex its muscles at the top end of the free-agent market; that if you're rich, you should be spending lavishly. There's logic to that (hello, Gerrit Cole), but the Yankees should be all about leveraging their immense resources to build the most devastating roster possible, one through 26. The name of the game should be quality depth. Instead of shopping at Bloomingdale's for nice accessories, the Yankees have been looking through the bargain bins at Kohls for costume jewelry.

Even in an offseason where they acquired one of the best pitchers in the world, the team refused to add at the margins. Instead, they relied on the "Next Man Up" squad from 2019 and suffered the consequences. In 2020, the quintet of Ford, Tyler Wade, Mike Tauchman, Miguel Andújar and Thairo Estrada combined for 0.1 Wins Above Replacement Player. If you compare that with a 2.6 WARP in 2019, the drop-off in production was stark. That lack of productive depth ended up playing a significant role in their inconsistent season.

Of course, no one knew a pandemic was on the horizon. But the Yankees knew more than anyone how important it was to have a deep, quality roster after the injury-marred year of 2019. They chose trust over opportunity, banking on those players repeating their previous performance. That they failed was somewhat predictable: benches over 60-game stretches are like bullpens when it comes to variance. There wasn't enough time for slumps to be worked through, for variance to be overcome. The best route was to acquire as much talent as possible and trust that it'll work out in the end. The Yankees didn't follow that route to roster-building.

After letting incumbent shortstop Didi Gregorius walk in free agency, the position was given to handpicked-successor Gleyber Torres. There's nothing wrong with this choice unto itself, but their refusal to restock the depth from which Torres emerged meant there was no stemming the upcoming ripple effect.

They instead found themselves overly reliant on the likes of Wade, your typical glove-first, bat second spare infielder (and a lightning rod for some feisty online Yankees fans). Instead of positioning him as a perfectly serviceable "break glass in case of an emergency" option, the Yankees treated him as a necessity.

As was the case in 2019, the injury bug took residence in the Yankees clubhouse and Wade ended up appearing in 87 percent of the squad's games, many of which saw him masquerade as a starter on a team with championship aspirations. Predictably, the Yankees suffered from inconsistency: they were in the midst of at least a five-game winning or losing streak in half their games.

That inconsistency didn't just lie at the feet of shallow position player depth. The pitching suffered from attrition as well. Losing ace reliever Tommy Kahnle early in the season proved to be a major blow to the team, with the Yankees having to turn to the likes of Jonathan Holder, Nick Nelson, Ben Heller, Tyler Lyons and Miguel Yajúre to shoulder the load. One can only wonder how things might have played out in Game 5 if Kahnle had been healthy. Or if more quality depth had been on-hand.

⚾ ⚾ ⚾

This brings us back to the issue of title windows for the Yankees. The organization willingly chose to rely upon Ford, Wade and the since-non-tendered Holder. Over the last 18 months, the team has made one significant addition: Gerrit Cole. Two trading seasons have passed wherein the Yankees were unable to deliver depth pieces. As of press time, it looks likely that the team will bring most of the old gang back to make another run at a title.

The Yankees' issues extend beyond available resources. Rather, this offseason is the culmination of a philosophy that limits the maximum potential for the team's core. With Aaron Judge, Sánchez and Torres getting closer to bigger paydays, the urgency to win a title in 2021 is greater than ever for this group. That task is much more difficult to achieve when strategy is to make the postseason and then hope for the best.

This hope brings us back to the night The Smirk of Chapman™ reared its ugly head. In a vacuum, the Brosseau home run was a thrilling moment of baseball theater. In a broader context, it signals a transition Yankees fans may struggle to acknowledge: The Yankees are replacing the Dodgers as the exceptional, brand name franchise that struggles to seal the deal.

The irony is Andrew Friedman, the Rays' original architect, was the one delivering a championship to L.A. The difference between the Yankees and Friedman's Dodgers lies in the overall depth manager Dave Roberts was able to wield. Under Friedman, the Dodgers have created a player acquisition philosophy requiring solid contributions across the roster—and even into the reserves. The Dodgers fill their roster with capable players, not just warm bodies. That spot is not a rotating formality based on available player options; on any given day, it can belong to former veteran starters who had been upgraded upon, like Chris Taylor and AJ Pollock, or more inexperienced players who hadn't yet worked themselves into expanded roles, such as Edwin Ríos. The bench isn't an afterthought, a last resort; it's part of the championship formula.

The Smirk of Chapman™, then, is the embodiment of these Yankees. Despite being blessed beyond belief, their fate has been decided and defined by the margins—be it the location of a fastball on the field, or the placement of a comma on a ledger that steers them away from leveraging their greatest strength: their financial might. The difference between a smile and a smirk is a matter of degrees; the difference between the Yankees and Dodgers is, too.

—*Randy Wilkins is a filmmaker and co-founder of the New York Yankees blog Views From 314ft.*

Part 2: Player Analysis

PLAYER COMMENTS WITH GRAPHS

Miguel Andújar 3B
Born: 03/02/95   Age: 26   Bats: R   Throws: R
Height: 6'0"   Weight: 211   Origin: International Free Agent, 2011

YEAR	TEAM	LVL	AGE	PA	R	2B	3B	HR	RBI	BB	K	SB	CS	AVG/OBP/SLG
2018	NYY	MLB	23	606	83	47	2	27	92	25	97	2	1	.297/.328/.527
2019	NYY	MLB	24	49	1	0	0	0	1	1	11	0	0	.128/.143/.128
2020	NYY	MLB	25	65	5	2	1	1	5	3	9	0	0	.242/.277/.355
2021 FS	NYY	MLB	26	600	75	30	1	23	85	32	111	1	1	.265/.311/.450
2021 DC	NYY	MLB	26	166	21	8	0	6	23	8	30	0	0	.265/.311/.450

Comparables: Danny Valencia, Jorge Cantu, Manny Machado

    Andújar nearly won the Rookie of the Year Award in 2018. He's now been an afterthought for the Yankees in the two seasons since. It wasn't because of injury this time; rather, it was because New York needed pitching more than it needed hitting. As a result, the Yankees couldn't find space for him, even on a 28-player roster. On another squad, there would be a place for Andújar's bat, defensive limitations and all; the Yankees, though, already have too many old and injury-susceptible players who need to rotate in at DH. A change of scenery seems inevitable; especially after Andújar's agent complained in September that his client was unfairly and undeservedly demoted.

YEAR	TEAM	LVL	AGE	PA	DRC+	BABIP	BRR	FRAA	WARP
2018	NYY	MLB	23	606	119	.316	-0.1	3B(136): -15.2	2.0
2019	NYY	MLB	24	49	62	.162	0.2	3B(4): -0.8	-0.2
2020	NYY	MLB	25	65	83	.269	0.5	LF(7): -0.6, 3B(6): -0.5	-0.1
2021 FS	NYY	MLB	26	600	106	.295	-0.9	3B -1, LF -4	1.0
2021 DC	NYY	MLB	26	166	106	.295	-0.2	3B 0, LF -1	0.3

Miguel Andújar, continued

Batted Ball Distribution

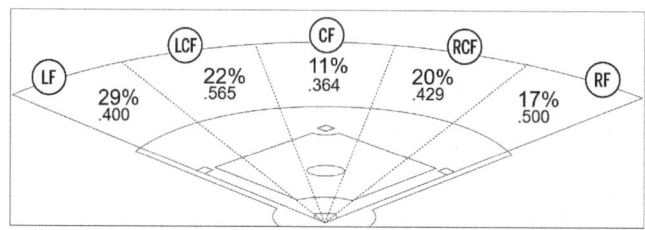

Strike Zone vs LHP   Strike Zone vs RHP

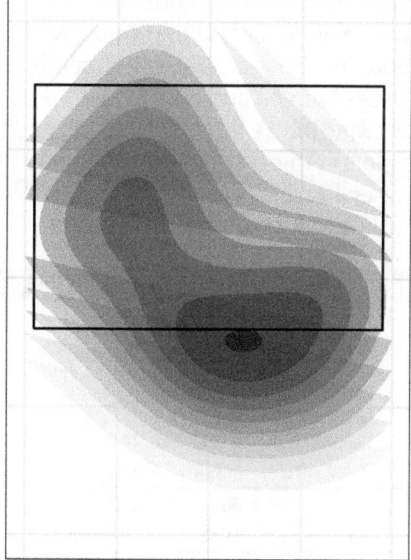

Clint Frazier RF

Born: 09/06/94   Age: 26   Bats: R   Throws: R
Height: 5'11"   Weight: 212   Origin: Round 1, 2013 Draft (#5 overall)

YEAR	TEAM	LVL	AGE	PA	R	2B	3B	HR	RBI	BB	K	SB	CS	AVG/OBP/SLG
2018	TAM	HI-A	23	26	6	1	0	1	3	4	3	2	0	.250/.385/.450
2018	SWB	AAA	23	216	38	14	3	10	21	23	52	4	2	.311/.389/.574
2018	NYY	MLB	23	41	9	3	0	0	1	5	13	0	0	.265/.390/.353
2019	SWB	AAA	24	269	35	20	1	8	26	17	56	1	2	.247/.305/.433
2019	NYY	MLB	24	246	31	14	0	12	38	16	70	1	2	.267/.317/.489
2020	NYY	MLB	25	160	24	6	1	8	26	25	44	3	0	.267/.394/.511
2021 FS	NYY	MLB	26	600	81	24	2	24	82	61	176	3	2	.234/.321/.429
2021 DC	NYY	MLB	26	507	68	20	2	20	69	51	149	2	2	.234/.321/.429

Comparables: Jay Buhner, Jorge Soler, Wily Mo Pena

Frazier not only emerged as the offensive force that once made scouts drool over his middle-of-the-order potential, he was even a defensive asset, grading out anywhere between above average or better depending on the metric. It turns out that Frazier was trying to play through post-concussion syndrome in 2019, which led to depth-perception issues and, in turn, tentative outfield play due to his fear of running into a wall. Labeled as soft and called malcontent entering the year, Frazier ultimately had a legitimate medical reason for his issues both on and off the field. He even turned things around with the press, drawing praise for his leadership and openness about wearing a mask on the field. Let this be a lesson about how the media needs to do better when assessing the impact of injuries, not only on a player's performance but on his attitude as well.

YEAR	TEAM	LVL	AGE	PA	DRC+	BABIP	BRR	FRAA	WARP
2018	TAM	HI-A	23	26	96	.235	0.3	LF(3): -0.3	0.0
2018	SWB	AAA	23	216	139	.380	0.9	CF(26): -2.9, LF(16): -0.3, RF(4): -0.3	1.0
2018	NYY	MLB	23	41	75	.429	0.2	LF(9): -0.7, CF(1): -0.2	-0.1
2019	SWB	AAA	24	269	80	.288	-0.8	LF(52): -0.1, CF(7): -1.3	-0.2
2019	NYY	MLB	24	246	99	.329	-0.6	RF(36): -1.7, LF(17): 0.5	0.4
2020	NYY	MLB	25	160	117	.338	2.0	RF(28): 1.4, LF(8): -0.2	0.9
2021 FS	NYY	MLB	26	600	104	.302	-0.4	LF 0, RF 1	1.9
2021 DC	NYY	MLB	26	507	104	.302	-0.3	LF 0, RF 1	1.5

Clint Frazier, continued

Batted Ball Distribution

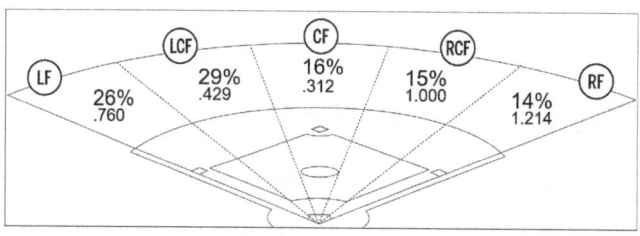

Strike Zone vs LHP **Strike Zone vs RHP**

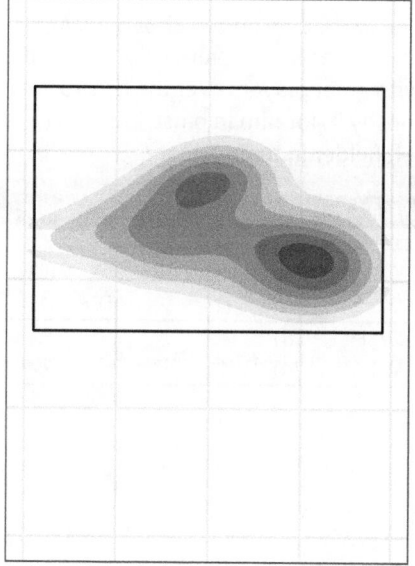

Brett Gardner CF

Born: 08/24/83 Age: 37 Bats: L Throws: L
Height: 5'11" Weight: 195 Origin: Round 3, 2005 Draft (#109 overall)

YEAR	TEAM	LVL	AGE	PA	R	2B	3B	HR	RBI	BB	K	SB	CS	AVG/OBP/SLG
2018	NYY	MLB	34	609	95	20	7	12	45	65	107	16	2	.236/.322/.368
2019	NYY	MLB	35	550	86	26	7	28	74	52	108	10	2	.251/.325/.503
2020	NYY	MLB	36	158	20	5	1	5	15	26	35	3	3	.223/.354/.392
2021 FS	NYY	MLB	37	600	67	22	3	19	69	69	140	16	5	.230/.328/.394
2021 DC	NYY	MLB	37	297	33	11	1	9	34	34	69	7	3	.230/.328/.394

Comparables: Gary Redus, Chuck Hinton, Trenidad Hubbard

"But then again, all good things must come to an end."

Q's premature farewell to Captain Jean-Luc Picard in *Star Trek: The Next Generation* will eventually apply to Gardner and his lengthy Yankee career. Even from the beginning, as a rookie in 2008, he was seen as less of a long-term solution and more of a stopgap while the Yankees found a superior option via trade or the free-agent market. Instead, Gardner not only persevered but thrived. His calling card was as one of the best defensive left fielders in baseball, and to that, he added above-average production with his bat and his consistency. He never performed like a superstar but, on a Yankees team filled with great players over the last 13 years, he never needed to. Even if this is it, or mostly it, for him in pinstripes, there's a case to be made for Gardner as the best left fielder in team history.

YEAR	TEAM	LVL	AGE	PA	DRC+	BABIP	BRR	FRAA	WARP
2018	NYY	MLB	34	609	90	.272	4.1	LF(107): 11.8, CF(34): -0.0	2.6
2019	NYY	MLB	35	550	109	.265	1.4	CF(98): 1.7, LF(45): -1.9	2.6
2020	NYY	MLB	36	158	110	.264	0.7	LF(39): -3.1, CF(10): 1.2	0.5
2021 FS	NYY	MLB	37	600	96	.279	1.0	LF 1, CF 1	1.8
2021 DC	NYY	MLB	37	297	96	.279	0.5	LF 1, CF 1	0.9

Brett Gardner, continued

Batted Ball Distribution

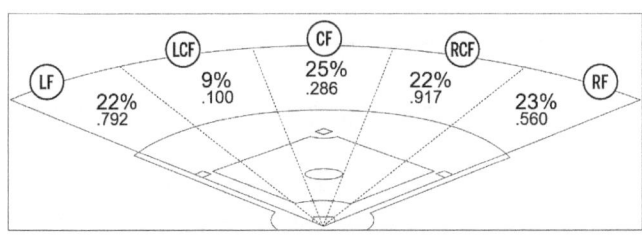

Strike Zone vs LHP   ### Strike Zone vs RHP

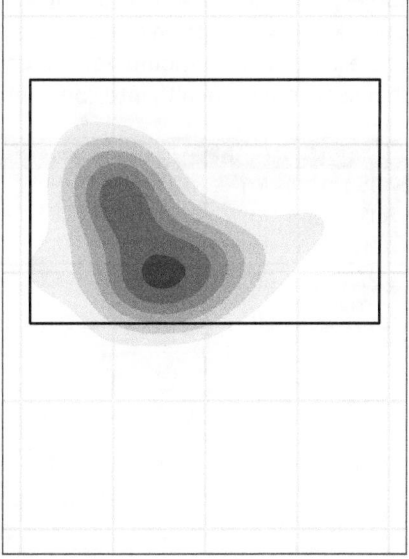

Aaron Hicks CF

Born: 10/02/89 Age: 31 Bats: S Throws: R
Height: 6'1" Weight: 205 Origin: Round 1, 2008 Draft (#14 overall)

YEAR	TEAM	LVL	AGE	PA	R	2B	3B	HR	RBI	BB	K	SB	CS	AVG/OBP/SLG
2018	NYY	MLB	28	581	90	18	3	27	79	90	111	11	2	.248/.366/.467
2019	NYY	MLB	29	255	41	10	0	12	36	31	72	1	2	.235/.325/.443
2020	NYY	MLB	30	211	28	10	2	6	21	41	38	4	1	.225/.379/.414
2021 FS	NYY	MLB	31	600	84	24	1	22	75	86	128	10	5	.238/.352/.422
2021 DC	NYY	MLB	31	571	80	23	1	21	71	82	122	9	5	.238/.352/.422

Comparables: Buddy Bradford, Milton Bradley, Carl Everett

For all we know about Tommy John surgery and its impact on pitchers, significant data gaps remain when it comes to hitters who undergo the procedure. In October 2019, Hicks opted to have the surgery on his throwing elbow. The delayed start of the 2020 season kept Hicks from missing any time, but the version of him who returned looked more like the hitter battling through discomfort in 2019 rather than the four-WARP outfielder he was in the previous seasons. Athletes are often seen as finely tuned machines, but recovery from surgery is mental as well as physical. Hitters coming back from Tommy John can take anywhere from one to three months to mentally adjust to their "new" bodies. Hicks' 2020 should not and can not be evaluated without taking that aspect of his health into consideration.

YEAR	TEAM	LVL	AGE	PA	DRC+	BABIP	BRR	FRAA	WARP
2018	NYY	MLB	28	581	120	.264	2.3	CF(131): -8.6	2.9
2019	NYY	MLB	29	255	99	.286	0.3	CF(58): -6.8	0.3
2020	NYY	MLB	30	211	124	.256	0.1	CF(50): -2.4	1.1
2021 FS	NYY	MLB	31	600	114	.276	0.1	CF -2	2.8
2021 DC	NYY	MLB	31	571	114	.276	0.1	CF -2	2.7

Aaron Hicks, continued

Batted Ball Distribution

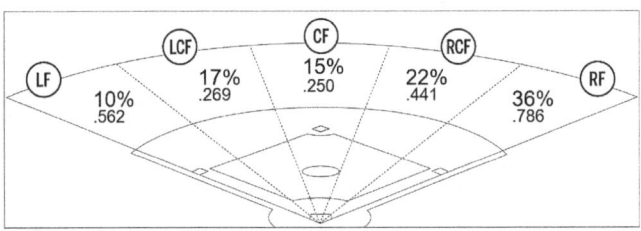

Strike Zone vs LHP   **Strike Zone vs RHP**

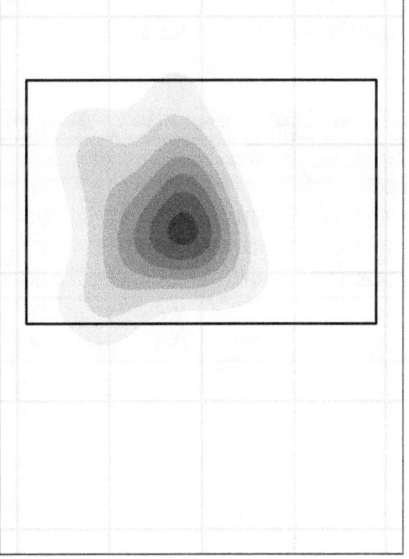

Kyle Higashioka C

Born: 04/20/90   Age: 31   Bats: R   Throws: R
Height: 6'1"   Weight: 202   Origin: Round 7, 2008 Draft (#230 overall)

YEAR	TEAM	LVL	AGE	PA	R	2B	3B	HR	RBI	BB	K	SB	CS	AVG/OBP/SLG
2018	SWB	AAA	28	211	16	10	1	5	22	17	44	2	0	.202/.276/.346
2018	NYY	MLB	28	79	6	2	0	3	6	6	16	0	0	.167/.241/.319
2019	SWB	AAA	29	270	42	13	0	20	56	24	53	0	0	.278/.348/.581
2019	NYY	MLB	29	57	8	5	0	3	11	0	26	0	0	.214/.211/.464
2020	NYY	MLB	30	48	7	1	0	4	10	0	11	0	0	.250/.250/.521
2021 FS	NYY	MLB	31	600	82	21	0	32	87	42	161	0	1	.225/.285/.442
2021 DC	NYY	MLB	31	186	25	6	0	10	27	13	50	0	0	.225/.285/.442

Comparables: Michael McKenry, Francisco Peña, Brett Nicholas

On September 16, Higashioka became only the third catcher in Yankees history (and the 38th backstop ever) to hit three home runs in a game. Despite the great day, and despite a higher WARP total than starter Gary Sánchez, Higashioka still profiles as a second stringer.

YEAR	TEAM	P. COUNT	FRM RUNS	BLK RUNS	THRW RUNS	TOT RUNS
2018	NYY	3438	3.2	0.8	-0.1	3.9
2018	SWB	6951	7.2	0.6	-0.2	7.6
2019	NYY	2271	1.9	0.1	-0.1	1.9
2019	SWB	9097	15.4	0.0	-0.1	15.4
2020	NYY	1794	1.5	0.1	-0.1	1.6
2021	NYY	7215	8.5	0.8	0.5	9.8
2021	NYY	7215	8.5	0.4	0.5	9.4

YEAR	TEAM	LVL	AGE	PA	DRC+	BABIP	BRR	FRAA	WARP
2018	SWB	AAA	28	211	60	.234	-0.7	C(49): 6.6	0.4
2018	NYY	MLB	28	79	98	.170	-0.7	C(27): 3.8	0.7
2019	SWB	AAA	29	270	122	.276	-3.2	C(64): 15.2	3.0
2019	NYY	MLB	29	57	62	.321	0.6	C(18): 2.1	0.3
2020	NYY	MLB	30	48	98	.242	-0.1	C(14): 0.1	0.3
2021 FS	NYY	MLB	31	600	93	.258	-1.0	C 24	4.3
2021 DC	NYY	MLB	31	186	93	.258	-0.3	C 10	1.6

Kyle Higashioka, continued

Batted Ball Distribution

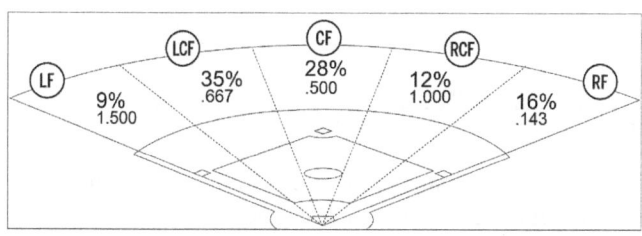

Strike Zone vs LHP   **Strike Zone vs RHP**

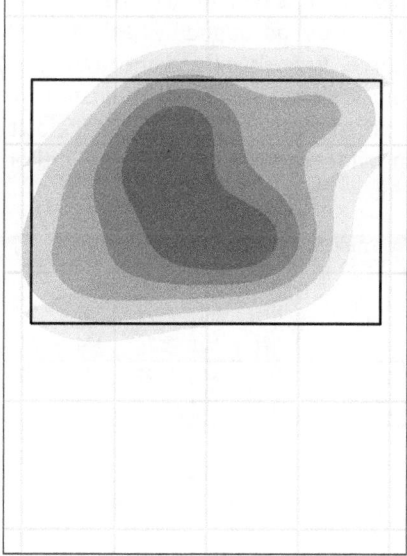

Aaron Judge RF

Born: 04/26/92 Age: 29 Bats: R Throws: R
Height: 6'7" Weight: 282 Origin: Round 1, 2013 Draft (#32 overall)

YEAR	TEAM	LVL	AGE	PA	R	2B	3B	HR	RBI	BB	K	SB	CS	AVG/OBP/SLG
2018	NYY	MLB	26	498	77	22	0	27	67	76	152	6	3	.278/.392/.528
2019	NYY	MLB	27	447	75	18	1	27	55	64	141	3	2	.272/.381/.540
2020	NYY	MLB	28	114	23	3	0	9	22	10	32	0	1	.257/.336/.554
2021 FS	NYY	MLB	29	600	103	22	1	37	94	81	193	5	2	.255/.365/.522
2021 DC	NYY	MLB	29	589	102	22	1	36	92	79	190	5	2	.255/.365/.522

Comparables: Giancarlo Stanton, Ryan Howard, Adam Dunn

    It would be easy when talking about Judge to start off by kvetching about the litany of injuries that have cost him a combined 138 games over the last three seasons. Be it the right calf strain that shelved him last year; the strained oblique in 2019; the chip fracture in his right wrist in 2018; and so on. Heck, this list doesn't even include the right shoulder and rib injuries last spring that would have landed him on the IL if the season had started on time. It is much more fun to focus on what you do get from Judge when he's on the field. Since his rookie season in 2017, he has been the best hitter in baseball not named Mike Trout as judged by DRC+. Even if you're not grading him on a per-at-bat curve, Judge has been one of the top 10 hitters in the game. The only Yankees outfielders with a higher adjusted-OPS in team history (minimum 1,500 PA) are named Ruth, Mantle and DiMaggio. It's best to appreciate what Judge does provide when he is on the field rather than lament what he could be because he sometimes isn't.

YEAR	TEAM	LVL	AGE	PA	DRC+	BABIP	BRR	FRAA	WARP
2018	NYY	MLB	26	498	137	.368	1.0	RF(90): 12.6, CF(1): -0.1	4.7
2019	NYY	MLB	27	447	131	.360	0.2	RF(92): 8.3	3.6
2020	NYY	MLB	28	114	110	.283	0.6	RF(25): 0.8	0.5
2021 FS	NYY	MLB	29	600	138	.333	-0.5	RF 7, CF 0	4.8
2021 DC	NYY	MLB	29	589	138	.333	-0.5	RF 6	4.7

Aaron Judge, continued

Batted Ball Distribution

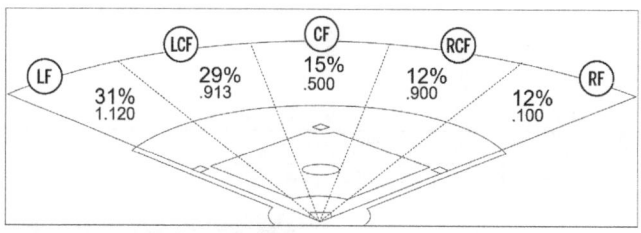

Strike Zone vs LHP   **Strike Zone vs RHP**

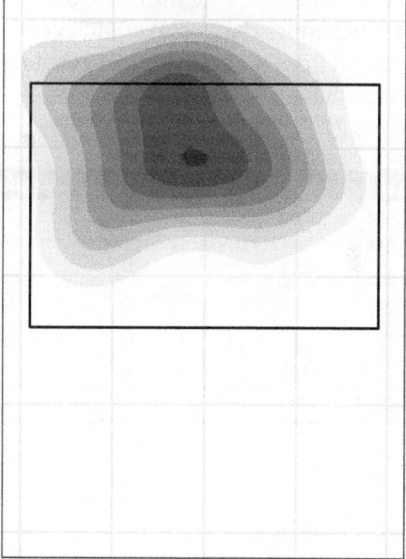

New York Yankees 2021

Erik Kratz C

Born: 06/15/80 Age: 41 Bats: R Throws: R
Height: 6'4" Weight: 250 Origin: Round 29, 2002 Draft (#866 overall)

YEAR	TEAM	LVL	AGE	PA	R	2B	3B	HR	RBI	BB	K	SB	CS	AVG/OBP/SLG
2018	SWB	AAA	38	61	10	2	0	4	6	7	10	0	0	.269/.356/.538
2018	MIL	MLB	38	219	18	6	0	6	23	6	40	1	0	.236/.280/.355
2019	SWB	AAA	39	176	27	10	0	7	31	17	21	1	0	.299/.375/.500
2019	SF	MLB	39	36	1	2	0	1	3	2	6	0	0	.125/.222/.281
2019	TB	MLB	39	17	0	0	0	0	0	0	8	0	0	.059/.059/.059
2020	NYY	MLB	40	30	2	2	0	0	4	2	6	0	0	.321/.367/.393
2021 FS	NYY	MLB	41	600	56	20	0	16	60	41	165	1	1	.198/.268/.328

Comparables: Henry Blanco, Pat Borders, Benito Santiago

Kratz announced his decision to retire early in the offseason. He drew rave reviews during his time with the Yankees for his mentoring of their minor-league staffs, particularly their Latinx hurlers. It's clear that he offered so much more than what could ever be gleaned from his statistics, and that he should have a future as a coach if he wants it.

YEAR	TEAM	P. COUNT	FRM RUNS	BLK RUNS	THRW RUNS	TOT RUNS
2018	MIL	8285	9.9	1.3	-0.1	11.1
2018	SWB	2267	1.1	0.3	0.0	1.4
2019	TB	666	0.4	-1.0	0.0	-0.7
2019	SF	1470	0.8	0.0	0.0	0.8
2019	SWB	5201	2.5	0.0	0.4	2.8
2020	NYY	1206	0.3	0.1	0.0	0.3
2021	NYY	16650	6.9	0.9	0.2	8.0
2021	NYY	16650	6.9	-0.7	0.2	6.4

YEAR	TEAM	LVL	AGE	PA	DRC+	BABIP	BRR	FRAA	WARP
2018	SWB	AAA	38	61	127	.263	0.0	C(17): 1.6	0.6
2018	MIL	MLB	38	219	90	.264	0.6	C(61): 10.2, P(3): 0.1, 1B(1): -0.0	2.0
2019	SWB	AAA	39	176	122	.305	1.2	C(37): 2.9, 1B(2): -0.2	1.5
2019	SF	MLB	39	36	72	.120	-1.2	C(11): 1.2	0.1
2019	TB	MLB	39	17	37	.111	-0.1	C(6): -0.7	-0.1
2020	NYY	MLB	40	30	89	.409	-0.2	C(12): -0.1, 1B(4): 0.0, P(2): 0.1	0.1
2021 FS	NYY	MLB	41	600	62	.251	-0.9	C 7, 1B 0	0.1

Erik Kratz, continued

Batted Ball Distribution

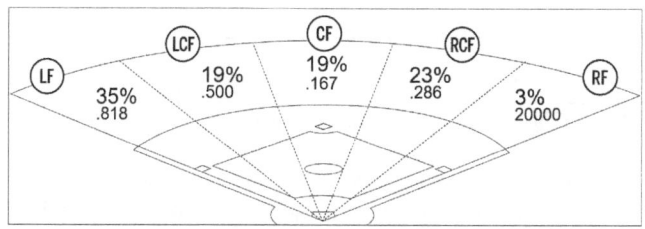

Strike Zone vs LHP   **Strike Zone vs RHP**

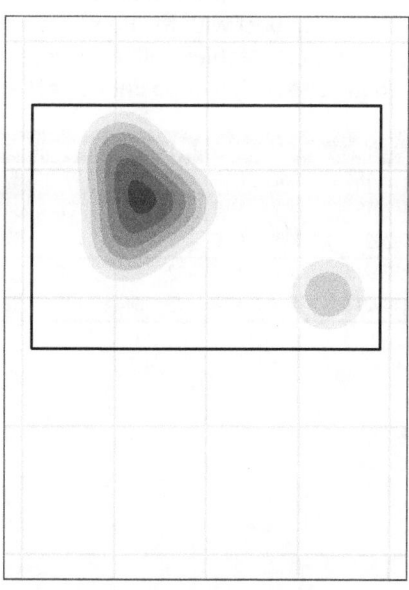

Type	Frequency	Velocity	H Movement	V Movement
● Fastball	55.3%	78.8 [56]	-7.4 [97]	-23.2 [77]
✱ Knuckleball	44.7%	61 [111]	0 [89]	-67.2 [111]

DJ LeMahieu 2B

Born: 07/13/88   Age: 32   Bats: R   Throws: R
Height: 6'4"   Weight: 220   Origin: Round 2, 2009 Draft (#79 overall)

YEAR	TEAM	LVL	AGE	PA	R	2B	3B	HR	RBI	BB	K	SB	CS	AVG/OBP/SLG
2018	COL	MLB	29	580	90	32	2	15	62	37	82	6	5	.276/.321/.428
2019	NYY	MLB	30	655	109	33	2	26	102	46	90	5	2	.327/.375/.518
2020	NYY	MLB	31	216	41	10	2	10	27	18	21	3	0	.364/.421/.590
2021 FS	NYY	MLB	32	600	96	25	1	18	65	51	88	7	4	.295/.360/.450
2021 DC	NYY	MLB	32	644	103	27	1	19	70	54	95	7	5	.295/.360/.450

Comparables: Brandon Phillips, Adam Kennedy, Omar Infante

Media members and fans alike spent more time in 2020 spilling virtual ink and weeping over the losses of Aaron Judge and Giancarlo Stanton to injuries, but it was LeMahieu's thumb sprain on August 15 that should have had Yankees' rooters holding their collective breath. While LeMahieu missed only two weeks (and nine games) because of the sprain, in a compressed 60-game season, his absence loomed large. Others have bigger names and brighter stars, but make no mistake that he has been the Yankees' best player since he signed a two-year, $24 million pact with the Bombers prior to the '19 season. A free agent as of press time, LeMahieu will be an asset in 2021 wherever he plies his trade at whatever position or positions he is asked to play.

YEAR	TEAM	LVL	AGE	PA	DRC+	BABIP	BRR	FRAA	WARP
2018	COL	MLB	29	580	97	.298	4.5	2B(128): 20.1	4.2
2019	NYY	MLB	30	655	127	.349	-2.1	2B(75): 4.5, 3B(52): 0.7, 1B(40): 1.5	4.8
2020	NYY	MLB	31	216	134	.370	-0.3	2B(37): 4.7, 1B(11): -0.3, 3B(11): -0.5	1.9
2021 FS	NYY	MLB	32	600	122	.326	-0.2	2B 8, 3B 0	4.1
2021 DC	NYY	MLB	32	644	122	.326	-0.2	2B 8, 3B 0	4.6

DJ LeMahieu, continued

Batted Ball Distribution

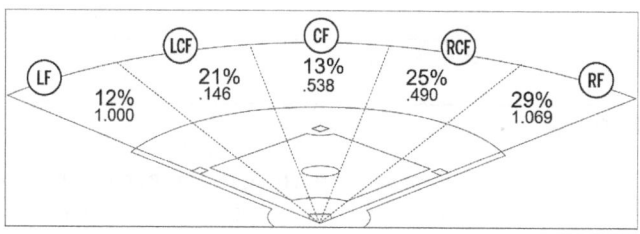

Strike Zone vs LHP   Strike Zone vs RHP

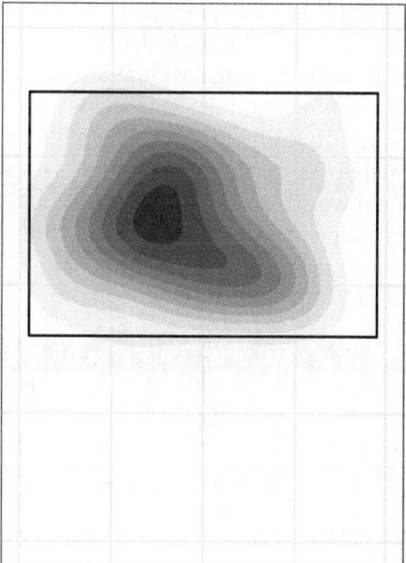

Giancarlo Stanton LF

Born: 11/08/89   Age: 31   Bats: R   Throws: R
Height: 6'6"   Weight: 245   Origin: Round 2, 2007 Draft (#76 overall)

YEAR	TEAM	LVL	AGE	PA	R	2B	3B	HR	RBI	BB	K	SB	CS	AVG/OBP/SLG
2018	NYY	MLB	28	705	102	34	1	38	100	70	211	5	0	.266/.343/.509
2019	NYY	MLB	29	72	8	3	0	3	13	12	24	0	0	.288/.403/.492
2020	NYY	MLB	30	94	12	7	0	4	11	15	27	1	1	.250/.387/.500
2021 FS	NYY	MLB	31	600	88	22	0	33	91	73	189	2	1	.232/.335/.469
2021 DC	NYY	MLB	31	521	76	19	0	28	79	63	164	2	1	.232/.335/.469

Comparables: Danny Tartabull, Tim Salmon, Reggie Jackson

In the film *Palm Springs*, Nyles is a man who gets trapped reliving the same day repeatedly while attending a destination wedding. Stanton must feel a little bit like Nyles, as he has spent nearly every day of his last two years as a Yankee either injured or answering the same tired questions about his most recent malady. He spent the offseason working diligently to maintain his health through a rigorous strength and conditioning program, but it couldn't prevent him from a strained right calf in late February that would put him on the shelf if the season had opened on time. He was able to take the field for the revised July opener, but it took all of 17 days for him to get hurt again; this time, a strained hamstring cost him a little over a month. Nyles eventually escaped his fourth dimensional prison thanks to his friend's dogged determination to teach herself quantum physics. There is no wormhole or magical portal that can change Stanton's trajectory, unfortunately. Instead, Stanton is relegated to our linear world, where his body will continue to age and his potential for physical breakdowns will increase. Here's hoping he can figure out a way to beat back against that reality sooner than later; lest we be robbed of even more of his prime.

YEAR	TEAM	LVL	AGE	PA	DRC+	BABIP	BRR	FRAA	WARP
2018	NYY	MLB	28	705	116	.333	0.0	RF(37): -1.1, LF(36): -0.0	2.6
2019	NYY	MLB	29	72	87	.424	-0.3	LF(10): -1.3, RF(3): -0.4	-0.2
2020	NYY	MLB	30	94	98	.333	-0.6		0.1
2021 FS	NYY	MLB	31	600	117	.295	-0.8	LF -1, RF 0	2.6
2021 DC	NYY	MLB	31	521	117	.295	-0.7	LF 0	1.9

Giancarlo Stanton, continued

Batted Ball Distribution

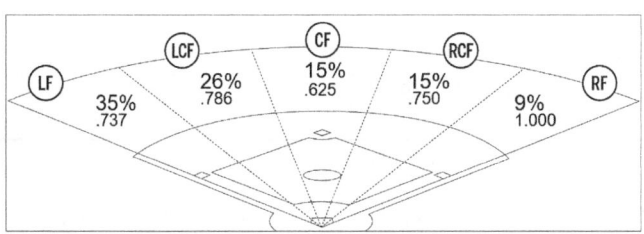

Strike Zone vs LHP **Strike Zone vs RHP**

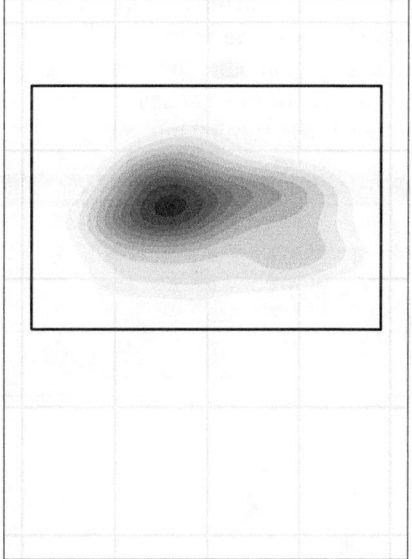

Gleyber Torres SS

Born: 12/13/96 Age: 24 Bats: R Throws: R
Height: 6'1" Weight: 205 Origin: International Free Agent, 2013

YEAR	TEAM	LVL	AGE	PA	R	2B	3B	HR	RBI	BB	K	SB	CS	AVG/OBP/SLG
2018	SWB	AAA	21	56	6	3	1	1	11	5	10	1	1	.347/.393/.510
2018	NYY	MLB	21	484	54	16	1	24	77	42	122	6	2	.271/.340/.480
2019	NYY	MLB	22	604	96	26	0	38	90	48	129	5	2	.278/.337/.535
2020	NYY	MLB	23	160	17	8	0	3	16	22	28	1	0	.243/.356/.368
2021 FS	NYY	MLB	24	600	80	25	1	26	83	62	135	7	4	.261/.344/.463
2021 DC	NYY	MLB	24	576	77	24	1	25	79	59	130	7	4	.261/.344/.463

Comparables: Evan Longoria, Corey Seager, Hank Blalock

Torres started the season in a prolonged slump, slashing a woeful .231/.341/.295 before landing on the IL on August 21 with left hamstring and quad strains. When he returned on September 5, he looked a lot more like the hitter who had wowed all of New York in his first two seasons. Torres started wearing glasses without lenses–something he did in 2019 on occasion–and seemed more comfortable and relaxed behind the frames. While "Glasses Gleyber" is a fun angle, it's probably nothing more than a framing device. The real change came as Torres adjusted to pitchers throwing him less heat. The key to a lengthy and prosperous big-league career is being able to make those tweaks as the need arises. As such, we see no reason to change our expectations about Torres turning into a star.

YEAR	TEAM	LVL	AGE	PA	DRC+	BABIP	BRR	FRAA	WARP
2018	SWB	AAA	21	56	117	.400	0.1	3B(8): 0.6, 2B(3): 0.0, SS(3): 0.2	0.3
2018	NYY	MLB	21	484	120	.321	0.8	2B(109): 5.4, SS(21): 1.5	3.7
2019	NYY	MLB	22	604	124	.296	-1.0	SS(77): -1.4, 2B(65): -1.0	3.9
2020	NYY	MLB	23	160	111	.286	0.6	SS(40): -1.1	0.6
2021 FS	NYY	MLB	24	600	118	.305	-0.1	SS -1, 2B 0	3.1
2021 DC	NYY	MLB	24	576	118	.305	-0.1	SS -1	3.0

Gleyber Torres, continued

Batted Ball Distribution

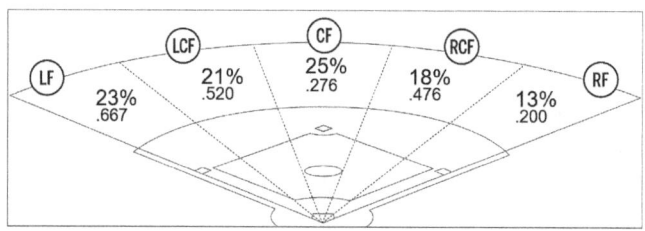

Strike Zone vs LHP

Strike Zone vs RHP

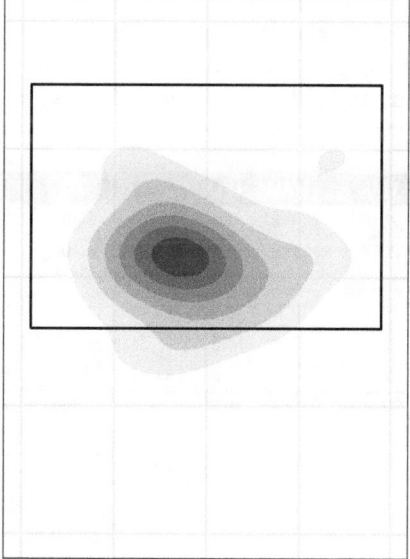

Gio Urshela 3B

Born: 10/11/91 Age: 29 Bats: R Throws: R
Height: 6'0" Weight: 215 Origin: International Free Agent, 2008

YEAR	TEAM	LVL	AGE	PA	R	2B	3B	HR	RBI	BB	K	SB	CS	AVG/OBP/SLG
2018	SWB	AAA	26	107	14	7	2	2	12	4	13	0	0	.307/.340/.475
2018	BUF	AAA	26	91	7	3	0	0	5	4	9	0	0	.244/.275/.279
2018	COL	AAA	26	42	6	4	0	0	7	5	9	0	0	.324/.405/.432
2018	TOR	MLB	26	46	7	1	0	1	3	2	10	0	0	.233/.283/.326
2019	NYY	MLB	27	476	73	34	0	21	74	25	87	1	1	.314/.355/.534
2020	NYY	MLB	28	174	24	11	0	6	30	18	25	1	0	.298/.368/.490
2021 FS	NYY	MLB	29	600	76	30	1	19	80	37	109	0	1	.268/.320/.431
2021 DC	NYY	MLB	29	559	71	27	1	18	74	34	101	0	1	.268/.320/.431

Comparables: Dave Roberts, Brent Morel, Charlie Hayes

No one is more emblematic of the Yankees' new way of doing things than Urshela, a player rejected by Cleveland and Toronto's organizations and who looked to be organizational filler at best when the Yankees purchased his contract in August 2018. Two years later, New York's low-end gamble on Urshela has paid off handsomely, as the club was able to coax more from his bat than anyone expected. A few years ago, the Yankees would have dumped millions on a competent but forgettable veteran (hello, Chase Headley). Now, it seems, they just unearth solid three-WARP players who let New York set it and forget it for years at a time.

YEAR	TEAM	LVL	AGE	PA	DRC+	BABIP	BRR	FRAA	WARP
2018	SWB	AAA	26	107	103	.337	0.0	3B(20): 1.1, SS(8): -1.0, 2B(1): -0.0	0.3
2018	BUF	AAA	26	91	104	.269	-0.1	3B(14): -1.4, 1B(7): 0.2, SS(2): 0.2	0.1
2018	COL	AAA	26	42	102	.429	0.3	2B(4): 0.3, 3B(4): 0.3, 1B(2): -0.3	0.1
2018	TOR	MLB	26	46	81	.281	-0.2	3B(10): -0.8, SS(8): -0.3	-0.1
2019	NYY	MLB	27	476	120	.349	-1.8	3B(123): 5.8, 1B(1): 0.0, LF(1): 0.0	3.4
2020	NYY	MLB	28	174	124	.315	-0.5	3B(43): 4.8	1.4
2021 FS	NYY	MLB	29	600	103	.303	-1.0	3B 2, 1B 0	1.6
2021 DC	NYY	MLB	29	559	103	.303	-0.9	3B 2	1.4

Gio Urshela, continued

Batted Ball Distribution

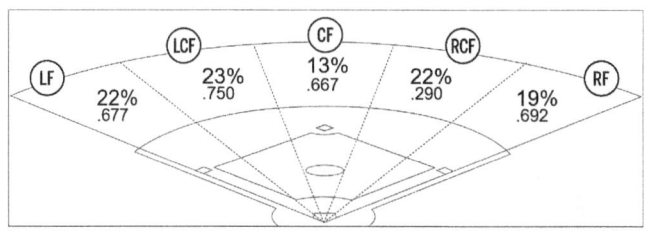

Strike Zone vs LHP   **Strike Zone vs RHP**

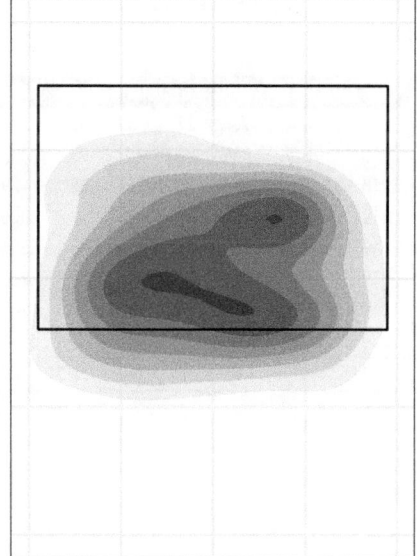

Andrew Velazquez 3B

Born: 07/14/94 Age: 26 Bats: S Throws: R
Height: 5'9" Weight: 170 Origin: Round 7, 2012 Draft (#243 overall)

YEAR	TEAM	LVL	AGE	PA	R	2B	3B	HR	RBI	BB	K	SB	CS	AVG/OBP/SLG
2018	MTG	AA	23	36	5	2	1	2	4	1	11	2	0	.229/.250/.514
2018	DUR	AAA	23	461	63	16	6	12	41	34	124	29	3	.258/.317/.409
2018	TB	MLB	23	12	3	1	0	0	0	1	3	1	0	.300/.417/.400
2019	COL	AAA	24	46	5	4	1	0	5	0	9	1	1	.244/.261/.378
2019	DUR	AAA	24	141	20	9	1	4	16	10	30	2	4	.271/.329/.450
2019	CLE	MLB	24	12	1	1	0	0	0	1	7	1	0	.091/.167/.182
2019	TB	MLB	24	12	2	1	0	0	0	0	6	0	0	.083/.083/.167
2020	BAL	MLB	25	77	11	1	1	0	3	10	23	4	2	.159/.274/.206
2021 FS	NYY	MLB	26	600	55	25	2	15	61	42	197	12	5	.214/.276/.351

Comparables: Josh Wilson, Brent Lillibridge, Robert Andino

Perhaps the biggest thing Velazquez brings to the table is "younger brother dragged along to a pick-up game" energy, in that he's a hard-nosed player who is often outclassed on the field. The good news? A recent article at FiveThirtyEight suggests that younger siblings end up the best athletes in the family.

YEAR	TEAM	LVL	AGE	PA	DRC+	BABIP	BRR	FRAA	WARP
2018	MTG	AA	23	36	80	.273	0.8	CF(7): 1.6	0.2
2018	DUR	AAA	23	461	95	.338	5.8	SS(69): -1.8, CF(33): 3.5, 2B(14): -0.7	1.7
2018	TB	MLB	23	12	88	.429	0.5	3B(4): -0.0, 2B(2): -0.0, SS(2): 0.1	0.1
2019	COL	AAA	24	46	78	.306	0.3	CF(6): 0.2, SS(5): -0.2, 2B(1): -0.1	-0.3
2019	DUR	AAA	24	141	75	.326	-1.0	CF(22): 3.5, SS(10): -1.1, 2B(1): 0.0	0.1
2019	CLE	MLB	24	12	25	.250	0.3	2B(3): 0.0, CF(2): -0.1	-0.1
2019	TB	MLB	24	12	67	.167	-0.5	3B(4): -0.6, 2B(2): 0.0, LF(1): -0.0	-0.1
2020	BAL	MLB	25	77	74	.250	0.7	SS(30): 1.0, LF(7): -0.1, CF(3): -0.0	0.1
2021 FS	NYY	MLB	26	600	68	.304	0.9	SS 0, CF 2	-0.3

Andrew Velazquez, continued

Batted Ball Distribution

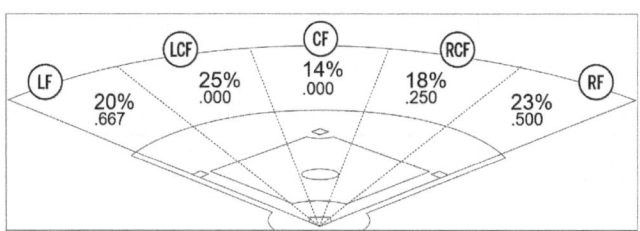

Strike Zone vs LHP   Strike Zone vs RHP

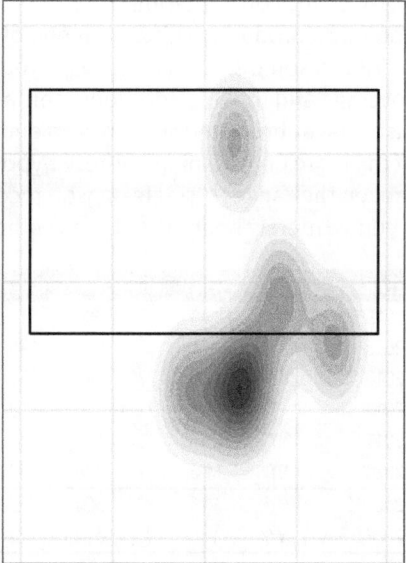

New York Yankees 2021

Luke Voit 1B

Born: 02/13/91 Age: 30 Bats: R Throws: R
Height: 6'3" Weight: 255 Origin: Round 22, 2013 Draft (#665 overall)

YEAR	TEAM	LVL	AGE	PA	R	2B	3B	HR	RBI	BB	K	SB	CS	AVG/OBP/SLG
2018	SWB	AAA	27	32	2	2	0	1	3	3	7	0	0	.310/.375/.483
2018	MEM	AAA	27	270	35	16	2	9	36	31	49	0	1	.300/.393/.502
2018	NYY	MLB	27	148	28	5	0	14	33	15	39	0	0	.333/.405/.689
2018	STL	MLB	27	13	2	0	0	1	3	2	4	0	0	.182/.308/.455
2019	NYY	MLB	28	510	72	21	1	21	62	71	142	0	0	.263/.378/.464
2020	NYY	MLB	29	234	41	5	0	22	52	17	54	0	0	.277/.338/.610
2021 FS	NYY	MLB	30	600	98	22	1	35	97	57	154	0	0	.263/.346/.508
2021 DC	NYY	MLB	30	614	101	22	1	36	100	58	158	0	0	.263/.346/.508

Comparables: Mike Napoli, Carlos Delgado, Cecil Fielder

So much time has been spent pontificating over whether or not Voit's Production is For Real that you'd think he's Bigfoot, El Chupacabra and The Loch Ness Monster all rolled into one. To be fair to the skeptics, Voit had the non-prospect, late bloomer, dragged-down-by-a second-half-injury in 2019 doubts all rolled into one entering last season. It turns out that when he's healthy, he's not only a productive hitter, but one of the most feared mashers in baseball. Voit sacrificed some selectivity for even more power in 2020, increasing his plate coverage and making additional contact thanks to his smart approach at the dish. The abbreviated season is an endless smorgasbord of "what ifs," and one of the more entertaining of these hypotheticals is wondering if Voit could have broken the Yankees' single-season record of 61 home runs. This only seems silly if you've merely heard the stories without experiencing it for yourself.

YEAR	TEAM	LVL	AGE	PA	DRC+	BABIP	BRR	FRAA	WARP
2018	SWB	AAA	27	32	118	.381	-0.1	1B(3): 0.2	0.1
2018	MEM	AAA	27	270	135	.347	-1.3	1B(56): 2.1, LF(1): -0.1	1.2
2018	NYY	MLB	27	148	155	.380	1.1	1B(32): -2.7	1.1
2018	STL	MLB	27	13	158	.167	0.1	1B(3): 0.3	0.2
2019	NYY	MLB	28	510	118	.345	-3.2	1B(83): -3.2	1.3
2020	NYY	MLB	29	234	132	.268	0.3	1B(48): -0.7	1.3
2021 FS	NYY	MLB	30	600	129	.308	-0.9	1B -1, LF 0	3.0
2021 DC	NYY	MLB	30	614	129	.308	-0.9	1B -1	3.0

Luke Voit, continued

Batted Ball Distribution

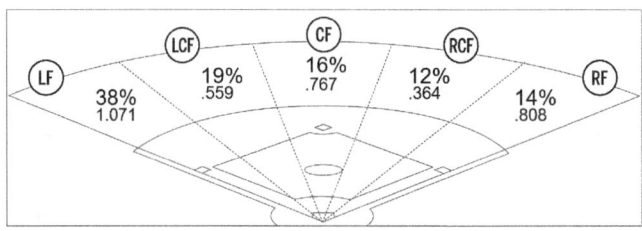

Strike Zone vs LHP   **Strike Zone vs RHP**

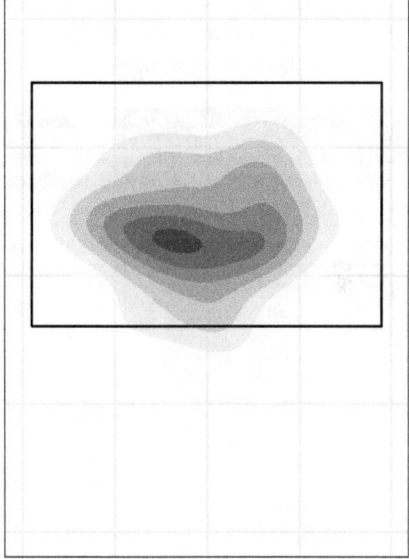

Zack Britton LHP

Born: 12/22/87   Age: 33   Bats: L   Throws: L
Height: 6'1"   Weight: 200   Origin: Round 3, 2006 Draft (#85 overall)

YEAR	TEAM	LVL	AGE	W	L	SV	G	GS	IP	H	HR	BB/9	K/9	K	GB%	BABIP
2018	BAL	MLB	30	1	0	4	16	0	15²	11	1	5.7	7.5	13	64.1%	.263
2018	NYY	MLB	30	1	0	3	25	0	25	18	2	4.0	7.6	21	77.8%	.229
2019	NYY	MLB	31	3	1	3	66	0	61¹	38	3	4.7	7.8	53	76.1%	.226
2020	NYY	MLB	32	1	2	8	20	0	19	12	0	3.3	7.6	16	71.7%	.226
2021 FS	NYY	MLB	33	2	2	7	57	0	50	44	3	4.8	8.8	48	70.8%	.293
2021 DC	NYY	MLB	33	2	2	7	56	0	55.3	49	4	4.8	8.8	54	70.8%	.293

Comparables: Anthony Bass, Tommy Hunter, Jeremy Jeffress

Thrust into the closer's role on Opening Day when Aroldis Chapman was sidelined with COVID, Britton did what he usually does: generate grounders with his mid-90s sinker and keep the ball in the yard. Since joining the Yankees, Britton has a 2.14 ERA, good for third-best all-time among pitchers with at least 100 innings thrown in pinstripes. He's lost a couple of ticks off his fastball since a 2018 injury, but has learned to thrive following an initial adjustment period thanks to increased use of a sharp-breaking curve that gives hitters a different look. The combination of worm burners and weak contact makes Britton a relief ace regardless of his assigned inning of work.

YEAR	TEAM	LVL	AGE	WHIP	ERA	DRA-	WARP	MPH	FB%	WHF	CSP
2018	BAL	MLB	30	1.34	3.45	172	-0.5	96.7	94.4%	35.0%	
2018	NYY	MLB	30	1.16	2.88	146	-0.5	96.7	93.1%	30.3%	
2019	NYY	MLB	31	1.14	1.91	71	1.2	96.1	86.1%	27.7%	
2020	NYY	MLB	32	1.00	1.89	81	0.4	96.3	80.3%	25.8%	
2021 FS	NYY	MLB	33	1.43	3.74	88	0.6	96.2	86.1%	28.1%	40.9%
2021 DC	NYY	MLB	33	1.43	3.74	88	0.6	96.2	86.1%	28.1%	40.9%

Zack Britton, continued

Pitch Shape vs LHH

Pitch Shape vs RHH

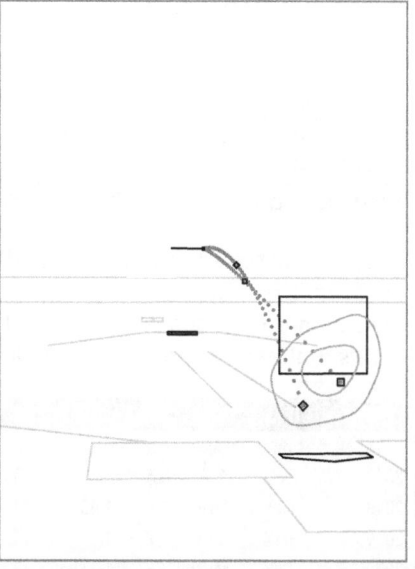

Type	Frequency	Velocity	H Movement	V Movement
☐ Sinker	80.3%	94.9 [113]	11.7 [110]	-22 [95]
◇ Curveball	19.7%	81.2 [110]	-8.8 [105]	-42.9 [112]

New York Yankees 2021

Luis Cessa RHP

Born: 04/25/92 Age: 29 Bats: R Throws: R
Height: 6'0" Weight: 208 Origin: International Free Agent, 2008

YEAR	TEAM	LVL	AGE	W	L	SV	G	GS	IP	H	HR	BB/9	K/9	K	GB%	BABIP
2018	TRN	AA	26	0	1	0	2	2	10	6	0	0.9	10.8	12	45.8%	.250
2018	SWB	AAA	26	3	0	0	6	5	26^1	19	1	1.4	8.5	25	39.7%	.250
2018	NYY	MLB	26	1	4	2	16	5	44^2	51	5	2.6	7.9	39	46.9%	.336
2019	NYY	MLB	27	2	1	1	43	0	81	75	14	3.4	8.3	75	48.3%	.277
2020	NYY	MLB	28	0	0	1	16	0	21^2	20	2	2.9	7.1	17	39.7%	.273
2021 FS	NYY	MLB	29	2	2	0	57	0	50	48	8	3.2	8.2	45	43.6%	.285
2021 DC	NYY	MLB	29	2	2	0	56	0	49.7	48	8	3.2	8.2	45	43.6%	.285

Comparables: Alex Colomé, Tyler Duffey, Trevor Williams

Cessa, who tested positive for COVID-19 on July 4, rattled off a streak of eight consecutive scoreless appearances after settling in upon his return. In a year when innings were at a premium and the schedule was often tempest-tossed, Cessa's rubber arm and yeoman work in middle relief were essential.

YEAR	TEAM	LVL	AGE	WHIP	ERA	DRA-	WARP	MPH	FB%	WHF	CSP
2018	TRN	AA	26	0.70	2.70	33	0.4				
2018	SWB	AAA	26	0.87	2.73	53	0.8				
2018	NYY	MLB	26	1.43	5.24	72	1.0	96.9	41.8%	27.0%	
2019	NYY	MLB	27	1.31	4.11	98	0.5	96.2	41.9%	29.8%	
2020	NYY	MLB	28	1.25	3.32	119	0.0	95.2	31.1%	27.7%	
2021 FS	NYY	MLB	29	1.32	4.25	98	0.3	96.1	39.2%	28.8%	43.3%
2021 DC	NYY	MLB	29	1.32	4.25	98	0.3	96.1	39.2%	28.8%	43.3%

Luis Cessa, continued

Pitch Shape vs LHH   **Pitch Shape vs RHH**

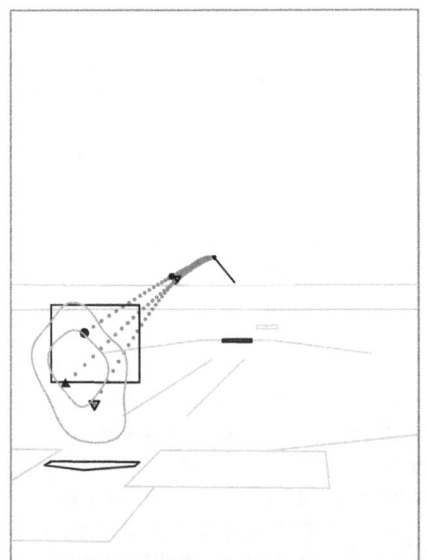 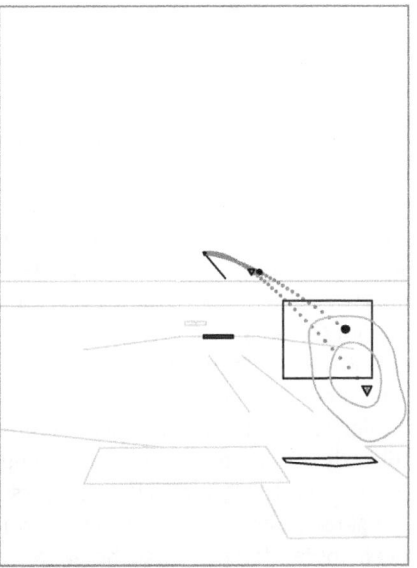

Type	Frequency	Velocity	H Movement	V Movement
● Fastball	19.7%	93.8 [104]	-6.2 [103]	-13.5 [105]
□ Sinker	11.4%	93.6 [106]	-12.2 [107]	-15.8 [115]
▲ Changeup	12.5%	87.7 [110]	-11.2 [103]	-24.7 [108]
▽ Slider	54.4%	83.8 [99]	2.8 [91]	-35.9 [94]

Aroldis Chapman LHP

Born: 02/28/88 Age: 33 Bats: L Throws: L
Height: 6'4" Weight: 218 Origin: International Free Agent, 2010

YEAR	TEAM	LVL	AGE	W	L	SV	G	GS	IP	H	HR	BB/9	K/9	K	GB%	BABIP
2018	NYY	MLB	30	3	0	32	55	0	51¹	24	2	5.3	16.3	93	46.4%	.268
2019	NYY	MLB	31	3	2	37	60	0	57	38	3	3.9	13.4	85	41.5%	.292
2020	NYY	MLB	32	1	1	3	13	0	11²	6	2	3.1	17.0	22	27.8%	.250
2021 FS	NYY	MLB	33	3	2	37	57	0	50	35	5	4.4	14.0	77	40.5%	.302
2021 DC	NYY	MLB	33	3	2	37	56	0	49.7	35	5	4.4	14.0	77	40.5%	.302

Comparables: Craig Kimbrel, Dellin Betances, Kenley Jansen

After missing nearly a month due to a positive COVID-19 diagnosis, Chapman shook off the rust and concluded the regular season with eight consecutive scoreless outings, allowing only three baserunners and fanning 17 batters. All fans will remember, though, is Chapman allowing the go-ahead and ultimately winning home run in the deciding Game 5 of the ALDS against the Rays, and Mike Brosseau triumphantly rounding the bases in the bottom of the eighth. That memory is inexorably linked to a particularly ugly incident from a month earlier, when Chapman cavalierly threw a 101 mile-per-hour fastball at or towards Brosseau's head, depending on who you believe. MLB was inclined to think it was the latter, as they only issued a three-game suspension for the dangerous pitch. There was a time when fans looked the other way and perhaps even applauded pitchers who engaged in a little chin music. That time has passed, and the near universal negative reaction to the incident is actually a good sign for the future of the sport.

YEAR	TEAM	LVL	AGE	WHIP	ERA	DRA-	WARP	MPH	FB%	WHF	CSP
2018	NYY	MLB	30	1.05	2.45	47	1.7	102.2	73.8%	37.4%	
2019	NYY	MLB	31	1.11	2.21	52	1.7	101.3	68.6%	31.8%	
2020	NYY	MLB	32	0.86	3.09	74	0.3	101.1	76.9%	41.6%	
2021 FS	NYY	MLB	33	1.20	2.85	68	1.1	101.5	71.4%	35.0%	48.7%
2021 DC	NYY	MLB	33	1.20	2.85	68	1.1	101.5	71.4%	35.0%	48.7%

Aroldis Chapman, continued

Pitch Shape vs LHH

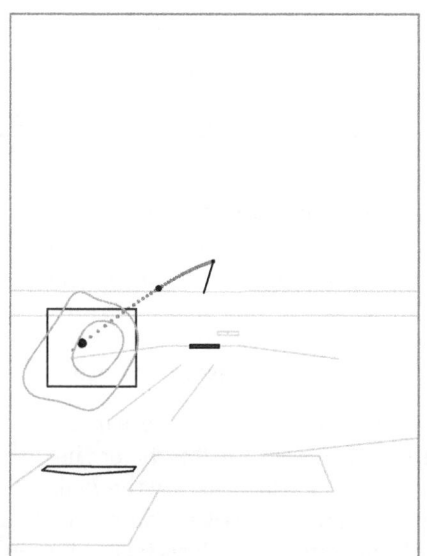

Pitch Shape vs RHH

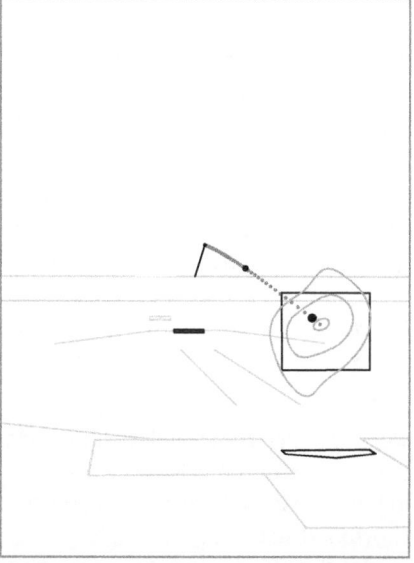

Type	Frequency	Velocity	H Movement	V Movement
● Fastball	72.9%	98 [117]	4.2 [112]	-9.1 [117]
☐ Sinker	4.0%	100.6 [142]	11.7 [110]	-10.4 [133]
▽ Slider	21.6%	85.3 [106]	-9.7 [117]	-30 [111]

Gerrit Cole   RHP

Born: 09/08/90   Age: 30   Bats: R   Throws: R
Height: 6'4"   Weight: 220   Origin: Round 1, 2011 Draft (#1 overall)

YEAR	TEAM	LVL	AGE	W	L	SV	G	GS	IP	H	HR	BB/9	K/9	K	GB%	BABIP
2018	HOU	MLB	27	15	5	0	32	32	200^1	143	19	2.9	12.4	276	36.3%	.288
2019	HOU	MLB	28	20	5	0	33	33	212^1	142	29	2.0	13.8	326	40.0%	.276
2020	NYY	MLB	29	7	3	0	12	12	73	53	14	2.1	11.6	94	37.1%	.242
2021 FS	NYY	MLB	30	10	6	0	26	26	150	118	21	2.5	11.8	196	39.0%	.287
2021 DC	NYY	MLB	30	14	7	0	30	30	193.7	152	27	2.5	11.8	254	39.0%	.287

Comparables: Cole Hamels, Kyle Hendricks, David Price

There was a great deal of concern over Cole's poor start after he signed a nine-year, $324 million deal that saw him receive the most guaranteed money ever handed to a pitcher (as well as the highest annual average value for any player in major league history). He wasn't bad, but a 3.88 ERA and nine home runs allowed in his first nine starts didn't align with the ace-level production that Yankees fans dreamed about following his introductory press conference.

Okay, take a breath and look carefully at the stat line above. Those marks were actually from Cole's first nine starts of 2019 with the Astros, before he became the apple in New York's eye, not his first nine in 2020 with the Yankees. In both seasons, Cole was fine; he just ran out of road in 2020 because of the shortened season. (Amusingly, he did perform better through his team's first 60 games than he did in 2019, posting an ERA over a full run lower.) It's a long contract, and maybe eight years from now, fans will be calling WFAN to yell about what a bum Cole was. For now, Year One of his Yankee tenure should be considered an unqualified success.

YEAR	TEAM	LVL	AGE	WHIP	ERA	DRA-	WARP	MPH	FB%	WHF	CSP
2018	HOU	MLB	27	1.03	2.88	56	6.4	98.7	56.4%	30.9%	
2019	HOU	MLB	28	0.89	2.50	48	7.9	99.3	54.0%	37.2%	
2020	NYY	MLB	29	0.96	2.84	79	1.5	98.6	52.8%	34.2%	
2021 FS	NYY	MLB	30	1.07	2.68	66	4.3	99.0	54.2%	34.9%	48.5%
2021 DC	NYY	MLB	30	1.07	2.68	66	5.5	99.0	54.2%	34.9%	48.5%

Gerrit Cole, continued

Pitch Shape vs LHH	Pitch Shape vs RHH
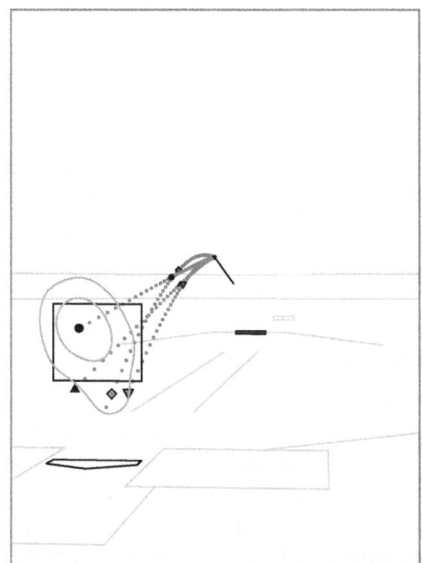	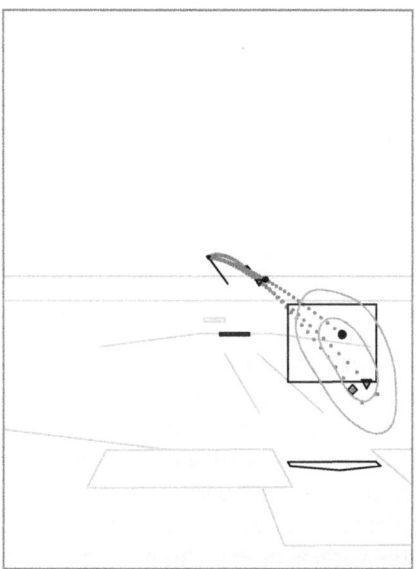

Type	Frequency	Velocity	H Movement	V Movement
● Fastball	52.8%	96.9 [114]	-10.9 [80]	-10.5 [113]
▲ Changeup	5.6%	88.5 [113]	-13.9 [89]	-22.1 [115]
▽ Slider	24.4%	88.9 [122]	4.5 [97]	-27.7 [118]
◇ Curveball	17.2%	83.5 [119]	8.4 [103]	-45.7 [106]

Deivi García RHP

Born: 05/19/99 Age: 22 Bats: R Throws: R
Height: 5'9" Weight: 163 Origin: International Free Agent, 2015

YEAR	TEAM	LVL	AGE	W	L	SV	G	GS	IP	H	HR	BB/9	K/9	K	GB%	BABIP
2018	CSC	LO-A	19	2	4	0	8	8	40²	31	5	2.2	13.9	63	27.5%	.310
2018	TAM	HI-A	19	2	0	0	5	5	28¹	19	0	2.5	11.1	35	35.4%	.297
2018	TRN	AA	19	1	0	0	1	1	5	0	0	3.6	12.6	7	37.5%	.000
2019	TAM	HI-A	20	0	2	0	4	4	17²	14	0	4.1	16.8	33	50.0%	.438
2019	TRN	AA	20	4	4	0	11	11	53²	43	2	4.4	14.6	87	40.5%	.363
2019	SWB	AAA	20	1	3	0	11	6	40	39	8	4.5	10.1	45	36.7%	.313
2020	NYY	MLB	21	3	2	0	6	6	34¹	35	6	1.6	8.7	33	34.0%	.293
2021 FS	NYY	MLB	22	9	8	0	26	26	150	135	26	3.5	10.1	168	37.0%	.290
2021 DC	NYY	MLB	22	7	6	0	22	21	115.7	104	20	3.5	10.1	130	37.0%	.290

Comparables: Bryse Wilson, Sixto Sánchez, Luis Severino

García had an outside chance to make the Yankees' Opening Day roster, but it wasn't until late August, when a pair of COVID-induced postponements turned the Subway Series into a frantic marathon of seven-inning doubleheaders, when García was summoned. While his debut against the Metropolitans was stellar, there were more downs than ups during his brief foray against major-league hitters. The numbers weren't great, but the observant eye could pick up on plenty of things to like: his deceptive delivery; the high spin rate on his curve; the vertical drop on his heater; and so on. García is also only 21 years old as of press time, so while 2020 wasn't littered with dominant performances, there is plenty of time for him to put it all together.

YEAR	TEAM	LVL	AGE	WHIP	ERA	DRA-	WARP	MPH	FB%	WHF	CSP
2018	CSC	LO-A	19	1.01	3.76	50	1.4				
2018	TAM	HI-A	19	0.95	1.27	65	0.7				
2018	TRN	AA	19	0.40	0.00	71	0.1				
2019	TAM	HI-A	20	1.25	3.06	72	0.3				
2019	TRN	AA	20	1.29	3.86	88	0.4				
2019	SWB	AAA	20	1.48	5.40	105	0.6				
2020	NYY	MLB	21	1.19	4.98	105	0.2	94.1	59.6%	22.8%	
2021 FS	NYY	MLB	22	1.29	4.18	95	1.8	94.1	59.6%	22.8%	49.8%
2021 DC	NYY	MLB	22	1.29	4.18	95	1.4	94.1	59.6%	22.8%	49.8%

Deivi García, continued

Pitch Shape vs LHH **Pitch Shape vs RHH**

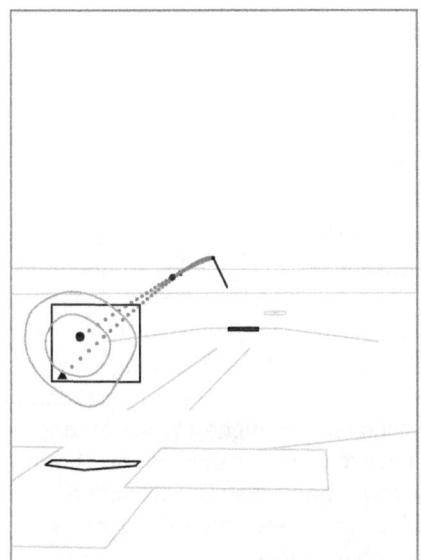 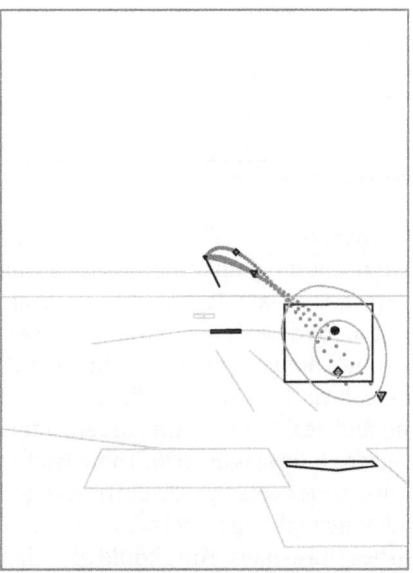

Type	Frequency	Velocity	H Movement	V Movement
● Fastball	59.6%	92 [98]	-7.5 [96]	-12.6 [107]
▲ Changeup	16.9%	80.7 [83]	-12.6 [95]	-27.5 [100]
▽ Slider	9.0%	82.6 [94]	4.4 [97]	-37.8 [88]
◇ Curveball	14.5%	75.4 [87]	7 [98]	-59.3 [76]

Chad Green   RHP
Born: 05/24/91   Age: 30   Bats: L   Throws: R
Height: 6'3"   Weight: 215   Origin: Round 11, 2013 Draft (#336 overall)

YEAR	TEAM	LVL	AGE	W	L	SV	G	GS	IP	H	HR	BB/9	K/9	K	GB%	BABIP
2018	NYY	MLB	27	8	3	0	63	0	75^2	64	9	1.8	11.2	94	32.4%	.307
2019	SWB	AAA	28	0	0	0	3	3	7^1	5	0	2.5	17.2	14	23.1%	.385
2019	NYY	MLB	28	4	4	2	54	15	69	66	10	2.5	12.8	98	35.5%	.346
2020	NYY	MLB	29	3	3	1	22	0	25^2	13	5	2.8	11.2	32	41.7%	.148
2021 FS	NYY	MLB	30	3	2	2	57	0	50	39	8	2.5	11.5	63	37.5%	.278
2021 DC	NYY	MLB	30	2	2	2	56	0	60.7	48	9	2.5	11.5	77	37.5%	.278

Comparables: Ken Giles, Raisel Iglesias, Chris Devenski

"Eat your greens" is a tired cliché nearly every kid has heard from their parents at the dinner table as they wanly pushed their vegetables around their plate, hoping a hole would open up and rescue them from their accursed fate. On a loaded Yankees squad, this Green is a bit like those boring vegetables in that he's not going to be the thing that gets you excited about coming to the table; he is, however, a solid part of any nine-inning meal and an integral part of the Yankees' menu. It was Green, after all, who had the highest WARP among Yankees relievers in 2020. There isn't any flash to Green's game, but his "boring" four-seamer gets the job done. And things have changed since you were a kid; they're doing all sorts of wonderful things with vegetable entrees and side dishes these days. You should give them another chance.

YEAR	TEAM	LVL	AGE	WHIP	ERA	DRA-	WARP	MPH	FB%	WHF	CSP
2018	NYY	MLB	27	1.04	2.50	75	1.3	97.5	86.6%	28.5%	
2019	SWB	AAA	28	0.95	2.45	42	0.3				
2019	NYY	MLB	28	1.23	4.17	76	1.3	98.0	77.1%	30.0%	
2020	NYY	MLB	29	0.82	3.51	85	0.4	96.8	75.1%	31.4%	
2021 FS	NYY	MLB	30	1.07	2.87	71	1.1	97.6	78.9%	30.0%	51.2%
2021 DC	NYY	MLB	30	1.07	2.87	71	1.3	97.6	78.9%	30.0%	51.2%

Chad Green, continued

Pitch Shape vs LHH

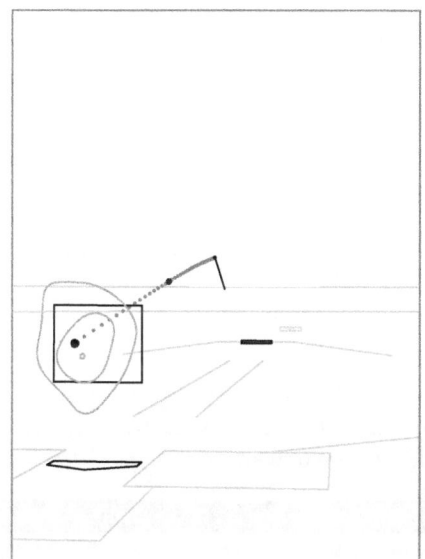

Pitch Shape vs RHH

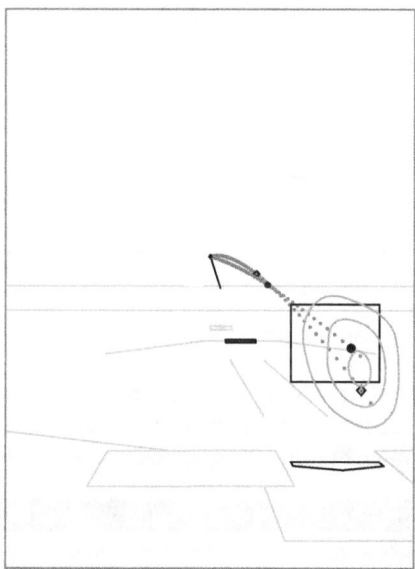

Type	Frequency	Velocity	H Movement	V Movement
● Fastball	73.4%	95.6 [110]	-4.9 [109]	-10.4 [113]
◇ Curveball	24.5%	84.6 [123]	3.3 [83]	-39.9 [119]

New York Yankees 2021

Michael King   RHP

Born: 05/25/95   Age: 26   Bats: R   Throws: R
Height: 6'3"   Weight: 210   Origin: Round 12, 2016 Draft (#353 overall)

YEAR	TEAM	LVL	AGE	W	L	SV	G	GS	IP	H	HR	BB/9	K/9	K	GB%	BABIP
2018	TAM	HI-A	23	1	3	0	7	7	40^{1}	33	1	2.2	10.0	45	58.9%	.305
2018	TRN	AA	23	6	2	0	12	11	82	65	4	1.4	8.3	76	44.7%	.279
2018	SWB	AAA	23	4	0	0	6	6	39	20	3	1.4	7.2	31	54.3%	.167
2019	YAW	ROK	24	0	0	0	3	2	5^{2}	3	0	3.2	12.7	8	75.0%	.250
2019	SI	SS	24	0	0	0	1	1	4	4	0	0.0	0.0	0	46.2%	.308
2019	TRN	AA	24	0	1	0	3	2	12^{2}	20	1	1.4	5.7	8	51.0%	.396
2019	SWB	AAA	24	3	1	0	4	3	23^{2}	20	3	2.3	10.6	28	47.5%	.293
2019	NYY	MLB	24	0	0	0	1	0	2	2	0	0.0	4.5	1	37.5%	.250
2020	NYY	MLB	25	1	2	0	9	4	26^{2}	30	5	3.7	8.8	26	40.2%	.325
2021 FS	NYY	MLB	26	9	8	0	26	26	150	146	23	2.4	7.7	129	42.8%	.287
2021 DC	NYY	MLB	26	5	3	0	32	6	65.7	64	10	2.4	7.7	56	42.8%	.287

Comparables: Sterling Sharp, Brandon Workman, Tyler Wilson

King's debut was his crowning achievement, but until he puts the finishing touches on his stuff, he's unlikely to dethrone any of the Yankees' front five. His reign of terrorizing opposing batters will just have to wait.

YEAR	TEAM	LVL	AGE	WHIP	ERA	DRA-	WARP	MPH	FB%	WHF	CSP
2018	TAM	HI-A	23	1.07	1.79	76	0.8				
2018	TRN	AA	23	0.95	2.09	69	2.0				
2018	SWB	AAA	23	0.67	1.15	77	0.8				
2019	YAW	ROK	24	0.88	4.76						
2019	SI	SS	24	1.00	0.00	117	0.0				
2019	TRN	AA	24	1.74	9.95	142	-0.3				
2019	SWB	AAA	24	1.10	4.18	61	0.8				
2019	NYY	MLB	24	1.00	0.00	106	0.0	92.8	65.9%	5.6%	
2020	NYY	MLB	25	1.54	7.76	106	0.2	94.8	65.7%	21.3%	
2021 FS	NYY	MLB	26	1.24	3.96	93	2.0	94.7	65.7%	20.4%	47.2%
2021 DC	NYY	MLB	26	1.24	3.96	93	0.7	94.7	65.7%	20.4%	47.2%

Michael King, continued

Pitch Shape vs LHH

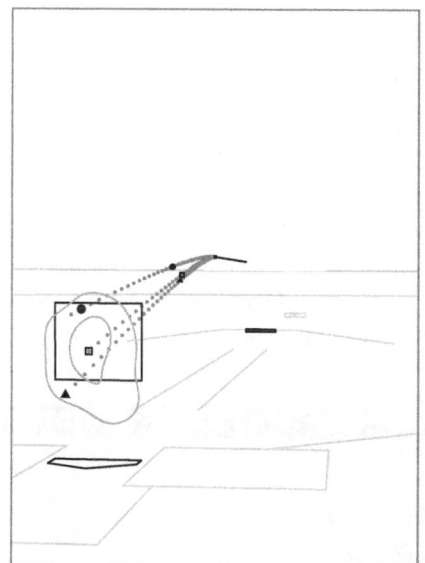

Pitch Shape vs RHH

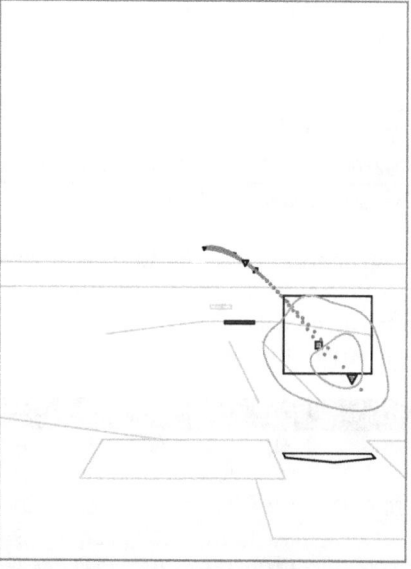

Type	Frequency	Velocity	H Movement	V Movement
● Fastball	7.9%	93.8 [104]	-9.1 [89]	-14.4 [102]
☐ Sinker	57.7%	93.1 [104]	-14.8 [87]	-21.4 [97]
▲ Changeup	14.9%	85.1 [100]	-14.5 [85]	-26.6 [103]
▽ Slider	19.4%	81 [87]	4.7 [98]	-39.5 [83]

New York Yankees 2021

Brooks Kriske RHP

Born: 02/03/94   Age: 27   Bats: R   Throws: R
Height: 6'3"   Weight: 190   Origin: Round 6, 2016 Draft (#188 overall)

YEAR	TEAM	LVL	AGE	W	L	SV	G	GS	IP	H	HR	BB/9	K/9	K	GB%	BABIP
2018	SI	SS	24	2	2	3	14	0	24²	21	0	2.9	12.0	33	45.5%	.396
2018	CSC	LO-A	24	0	0	0	2	0	4	4	0	2.2	13.5	6	0.0%	.444
2019	TAM	HI-A	25	1	1	1	7	0	12	4	0	3.8	12.0	16	38.1%	.200
2019	TRN	AA	25	2	2	11	36	0	48²	30	3	4.3	11.8	64	33.3%	.250
2020	NYY	MLB	26	0	0	0	4	0	3²	3	1	17.2	19.6	8	28.6%	.333
2021 FS	NYY	MLB	27	2	3	0	57	0	50	45	9	5.5	10.9	60	34.0%	.299
2021 DC	NYY	MLB	27	2	2	0	45	0	38.7	35	7	5.5	10.9	46	34.0%	.299

Comparables: Kyle Keller, Dany Jimenez, Zac Rosscup

An afterthought prior to 2019, Kriske moved up prospect lists after he added a few ticks to his fastball. He'll need to do a better job of commanding his three-pitch arsenal if he's to spare the world from learning if copy editors are willing to run "Kriske Kreme'd" headlines. (They are.)

YEAR	TEAM	LVL	AGE	WHIP	ERA	DRA-	WARP	MPH	FB%	WHF	CSP
2018	SI	SS	24	1.18	1.09	239	-1.8				
2018	CSC	LO-A	24	1.25	4.50	65	0.1				
2019	TAM	HI-A	25	0.75	0.00	53	0.3				
2019	TRN	AA	25	1.09	2.59	79	0.4				
2020	NYY	MLB	26	2.73	14.73	89	0.1	96.4	68.8%	39.1%	
2021 FS	NYY	MLB	27	1.52	4.98	108	0.0	96.4	68.8%	39.1%	39.1%
2021 DC	NYY	MLB	27	1.52	4.98	108	0.0	96.4	68.8%	39.1%	39.1%

Brooks Kriske, continued

Pitch Shape vs LHH

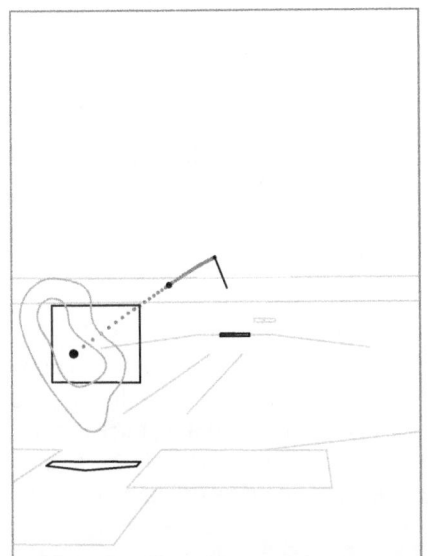

Pitch Shape vs RHH

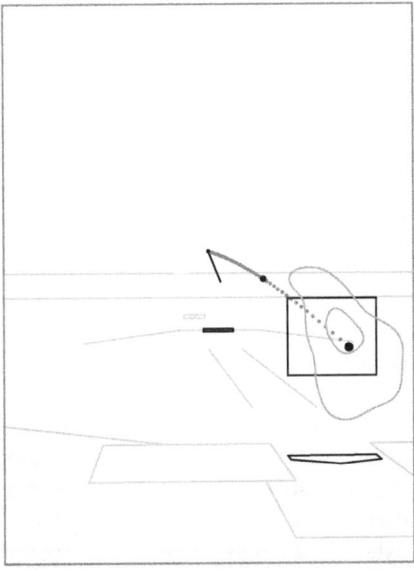

Type	Frequency	Velocity	H Movement	V Movement
● Fastball	68.8%	95 [108]	-6.3 [102]	-10.4 [113]
✕ Splitter	23.9%	85.7 [102]	-7.2 [103]	-30.6 [96]
▽ Slider	7.3%	83.2 [97]	2.9 [91]	-35.4 [95]

New York Yankees 2021

Jonathan Loaisiga RHP
Born: 11/02/94   Age: 26   Bats: R   Throws: R
Height: 5'11"   Weight: 165   Origin: International Free Agent, 2012

YEAR	TEAM	LVL	AGE	W	L	SV	G	GS	IP	H	HR	BB/9	K/9	K	GB%	BABIP
2018	TAM	HI-A	23	3	0	0	4	4	20	19	0	0.5	11.7	26	51.9%	.365
2018	TRN	AA	23	3	1	0	9	9	34^1	37	6	1.6	10.5	40	38.7%	.356
2018	NYY	MLB	23	2	0	0	9	4	24^2	26	3	4.4	12.0	33	52.4%	.383
2019	SWB	AAA	24	0	2	0	5	4	15^2	14	3	2.9	10.9	19	46.5%	.275
2019	NYY	MLB	24	2	2	0	15	4	31^2	31	6	4.5	10.5	37	40.0%	.316
2020	NYY	MLB	25	3	0	0	12	3	23	21	3	2.7	8.6	22	51.5%	.290
2021 FS	NYY	MLB	26	2	2	0	57	0	50	44	6	3.7	9.6	53	45.1%	.290
2021 DC	NYY	MLB	26	2	1	0	40	0	44	39	6	3.7	9.6	47	45.1%	.290

Comparables: Roberto Osuna, Alex Reyes, Ryan Helsley

Loaisiga has been called "Johnny Lasagna" since his early days as a professional, even though he hails from Nicaragua and his surname is of Spanish origin. The name Loaisiga derives from "Loyzaga", and there is a Loizaga Tower in Spain that stands to this day. The tower is now a museum that houses a collection of Rolls Royce vehicles, with 45 unique models dating back to the 1910 Silver Ghost. All of this is immaterial to Loaisiga's current and future status with the Yankees, but with some cursory research and just a smidgen of imagination, he could have a cool nickname like "Rolls" or "Silver Ghost" instead of a cheesy moniker that sounds like a bad stereotypical mafia name Martin Scorsese would have left on the cutting room floor.

YEAR	TEAM	LVL	AGE	WHIP	ERA	DRA-	WARP	MPH	FB%	WHF	CSP
2018	TAM	HI-A	23	1.00	1.35	76	0.4				
2018	TRN	AA	23	1.25	3.93	65	0.9				
2018	NYY	MLB	23	1.54	5.11	73	0.5	97.5	55.8%	30.6%	
2019	SWB	AAA	24	1.21	6.32	65	0.5				
2019	NYY	MLB	24	1.48	4.55	109	0.1	99.0	56.3%	33.2%	
2020	NYY	MLB	25	1.22	3.52	84	0.4	98.0	67.3%	23.2%	
2021 FS	NYY	MLB	26	1.30	3.87	90	0.5	98.3	60.8%	28.6%	47.1%
2021 DC	NYY	MLB	26	1.30	3.87	90	0.5	98.3	60.8%	28.6%	47.1%

Jonathan Loaisiga, continued

Pitch Shape vs LHH

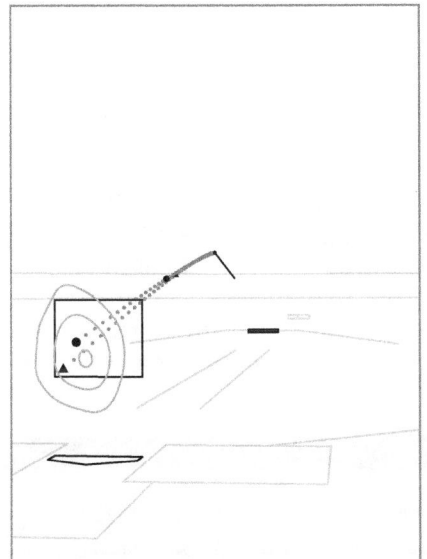

Pitch Shape vs RHH

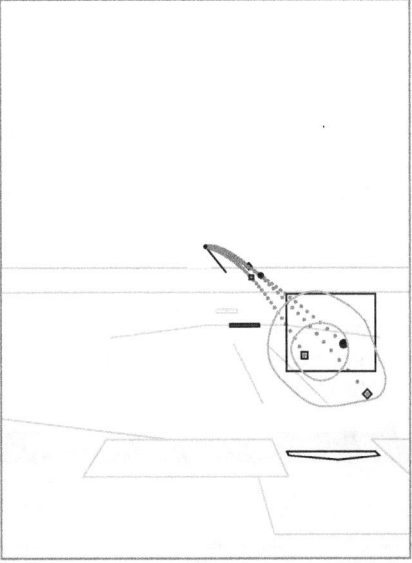

Type	Frequency	Velocity	H Movement	V Movement
● Fastball	43.2%	97 [114]	-5.2 [107]	-11.5 [110]
☐ Sinker	23.7%	96.4 [120]	-13.2 [99]	-15.5 [116]
▲ Changeup	15.2%	88.9 [115]	-13.5 [91]	-22.7 [113]
◇ Curveball	17.2%	83.9 [121]	9.3 [107]	-38.3 [122]

Jordan Montgomery LHP

Born: 12/27/92   Age: 28   Bats: L   Throws: L
Height: 6'6"   Weight: 228   Origin: Round 4, 2014 Draft (#122 overall)

YEAR	TEAM	LVL	AGE	W	L	SV	G	GS	IP	H	HR	BB/9	K/9	K	GB%	BABIP
2018	NYY	MLB	25	2	0	0	6	6	27¹	25	3	4.0	7.6	23	45.7%	.282
2019	NYY	MLB	26	0	0	0	2	1	4	7	1	0.0	11.2	5	21.4%	.462
2020	NYY	MLB	27	2	3	0	10	10	44	48	7	1.8	9.6	47	43.3%	.323
2021 FS	NYY	MLB	28	9	8	0	26	26	150	138	22	3.2	9.3	154	41.4%	.291
2021 DC	NYY	MLB	28	7	6	0	27	22	115.7	106	17	3.2	9.3	119	41.4%	.291

Comparables: Nick Pivetta, Daniel Mengden, Jakob Junis

After a long and difficult recovery from Tommy John surgery in 2018, Montgomery was finally able to take the hill and pitch a full season...or, at least, as "full" of a season as the year 2020 could provide. He initially looked shaky, but after shaking off the rust, Montgomery put together a solid string of starts in September that gave the Yankee faithful hope heading into the winter. Provided his command and velocity are back to stay, then there's a present and a future for Montgomery in the Yankees' rotation.

YEAR	TEAM	LVL	AGE	WHIP	ERA	DRA-	WARP	MPH	FB%	WHF	CSP
2018	NYY	MLB	25	1.35	3.62	131	-0.2	91.6	41.1%	23.5%	
2019	NYY	MLB	26	1.75	6.75	125	0.0	93.0	50.0%	28.9%	
2020	NYY	MLB	27	1.30	5.11	84	0.8	94.2	52.3%	28.2%	
2021 FS	NYY	MLB	28	1.28	3.78	90	2.3	93.7	50.4%	27.5%	47.0%
2021 DC	NYY	MLB	28	1.28	3.78	90	1.7	93.7	50.4%	27.5%	47.0%

Jordan Montgomery, continued

Pitch Shape vs LHH

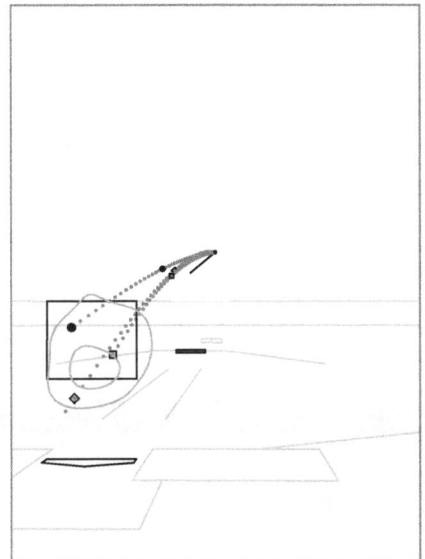

Pitch Shape vs RHH

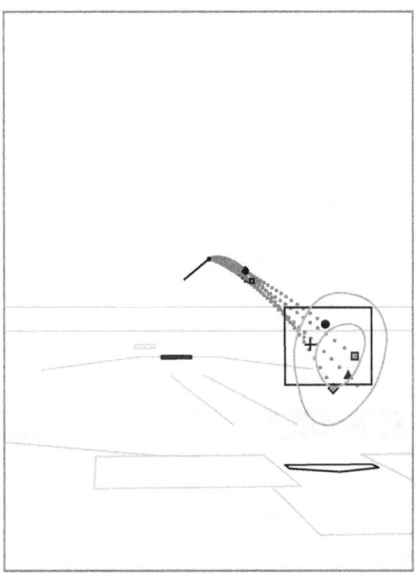

Type	Frequency	Velocity	H Movement	V Movement
● Fastball	20.2%	92.6 [100]	5.8 [104]	-14.2 [103]
□ Sinker	26.8%	92.6 [101]	12.9 [101]	-17.5 [110]
+ Cutter	5.4%	89.6 [108]	1.3 [79]	-19.2 [120]
▲ Changeup	25.6%	83.3 [93]	8.5 [117]	-22.4 [114]
◇ Curveball	22.1%	80.6 [108]	-1.1 [74]	-40.5 [118]

Nick Nelson RHP

Born: 12/05/95 Age: 25 Bats: R Throws: R
Height: 6'1" Weight: 205 Origin: Round 4, 2016 Draft (#128 overall)

YEAR	TEAM	LVL	AGE	W	L	SV	G	GS	IP	H	HR	BB/9	K/9	K	GB%	BABIP
2018	CSC	LO-A	22	1	1	0	5	5	24^2	18	1	2.6	12.8	35	50.9%	.309
2018	TAM	HI-A	22	7	5	0	18	17	88^1	69	1	4.8	10.1	99	44.9%	.302
2018	TRN	AA	22	0	0	0	3	3	8^2	10	1	9.3	10.4	10	50.0%	.360
2019	TAM	HI-A	23	0	0	0	1	1	3^2	4	0	2.5	17.2	7	57.1%	.571
2019	TRN	AA	23	7	2	0	13	12	65	48	4	4.8	11.5	83	31.1%	.301
2019	SWB	AAA	23	1	1	0	4	4	21	20	2	3.0	10.3	24	44.8%	.321
2020	NYY	MLB	24	1	0	0	11	0	20^2	20	4	4.8	7.8	18	55.7%	.281
2021 FS	NYY	MLB	25	2	3	0	57	0	50	46	7	5.0	9.6	53	42.1%	.297
2021 DC	NYY	MLB	25	1	2	0	40	0	44	41	6	5.0	9.6	47	42.1%	.297

Comparables: Adonis Rosa, Ryan Helsley, Jenrry Mejia

It was an underwhelming major-league debut for Nelson, but a 20-inning sample isn't enough to write off a pitcher with a hot fastball and three pitches.

YEAR	TEAM	LVL	AGE	WHIP	ERA	DRA-	WARP	MPH	FB%	WHF	CSP
2018	CSC	LO-A	22	1.01	3.65	74	0.5				
2018	TAM	HI-A	22	1.31	3.36	67	2.1				
2018	TRN	AA	22	2.19	5.19	81	0.1				
2019	TAM	HI-A	23	1.36	0.00	71	0.1				
2019	TRN	AA	23	1.28	2.35	95	0.3				
2019	SWB	AAA	23	1.29	4.71	56	0.8				
2020	NYY	MLB	24	1.50	4.79	93	0.3	97.9	57.2%	28.1%	
2021 FS	NYY	MLB	25	1.49	4.85	106	0.1	97.9	57.2%	28.1%	44.4%
2021 DC	NYY	MLB	25	1.49	4.85	106	0.1	97.9	57.2%	28.1%	44.4%

Nick Nelson, continued

Pitch Shape vs LHH	Pitch Shape vs RHH
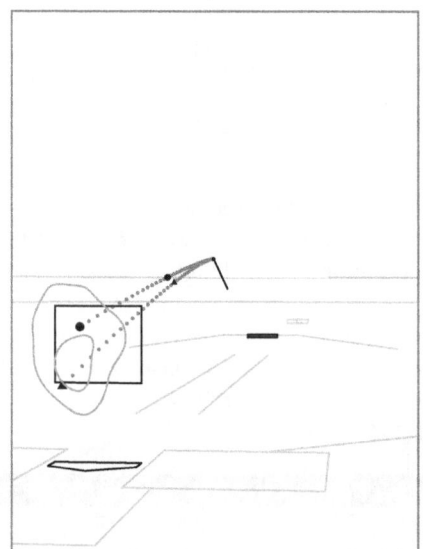	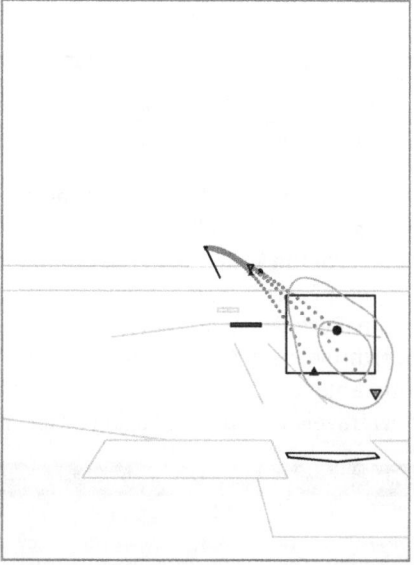

Type	Frequency	Velocity	H Movement	V Movement
● Fastball	57.2%	96.4 [112]	-6.8 [99]	-11.3 [111]
▲ Changeup	24.6%	88.7 [114]	-13.9 [89]	-26.4 [103]
▽ Slider	11.8%	84.7 [103]	9.9 [118]	-37.2 [90]
◇ Curveball	6.4%	79.9 [105]	8.7 [105]	-51.2 [94]

New York Yankees 2021

Darren O'Day   RHP

Born: 10/22/82   Age: 38   Bats: R   Throws: R
Height: 6'4"   Weight: 220   Origin: Undrafted Free Agent, 2006

YEAR	TEAM	LVL	AGE	W	L	SV	G	GS	IP	H	HR	BB/9	K/9	K	GB%	BABIP
2018	BAL	MLB	35	0	2	2	20	0	20	18	3	1.8	12.2	27	24.5%	.326
2019	ATL	MLB	36	0	0	0	8	0	5¹	3	0	1.7	10.1	6	23.1%	.231
2020	ATL	MLB	37	4	0	0	19	0	16¹	8	1	2.8	12.1	22	27.0%	.194
2021 FS	NYY	MLB	38	3	2	0	57	0	50	40	7	2.5	10.7	59	34.2%	.278
2021 DC	NYY	MLB	38	2	2	0	51	0	44	36	6	2.5	10.7	52	34.2%	.278

Comparables: Kyle Farnsworth, Dan Plesac, Pat Neshek

The year is 2048. Across the irradiated plains of the United States, desperate bands of survivors cling together and fight over access to water in the parched deserts of the Midwest. In the bombed-out remains of Washington, D.C., Emperor Barron Trump issues a decree condemning all haters and losers to death. Resistance fighters are preparing an offensive from New New York to overthrow his despotic regime. O'Day is wrapping up his 41st season on his 23rd different team as a middle reliever who handcuffs right-handers. His fastball now travels 72 mph. Opposing hitters bat .128 against it.

YEAR	TEAM	LVL	AGE	WHIP	ERA	DRA-	WARP	MPH	FB%	WHF	CSP
2018	BAL	MLB	35	1.10	3.60	82	0.3	88.1	52.1%	25.9%	
2019	ATL	MLB	36	0.75	1.69	103	0.0	87.8	55.1%	35.0%	
2020	ATL	MLB	37	0.80	1.10	90	0.2	87.2	57.1%	31.9%	
2021 FS	NYY	MLB	38	1.09	3.06	75	0.9	87.5	55.6%	30.8%	46.2%
2021 DC	NYY	MLB	38	1.09	3.06	75	0.8	87.5	55.6%	30.8%	46.2%

Darren O'Day, continued

Pitch Shape vs LHH

Pitch Shape vs RHH

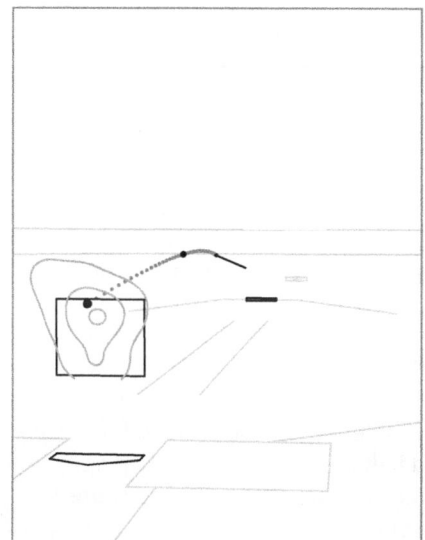
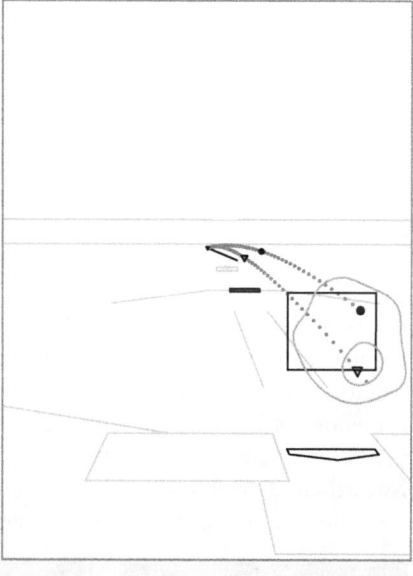

Type	Frequency	Velocity	H Movement	V Movement
● Fastball	46.4%	86.2 [80]	-10 [84]	-24.5 [74]
☐ Sinker	10.7%	85.9 [66]	-13.3 [98]	-34.7 [54]
▽ Slider	42.9%	78.5 [76]	7 [107]	-38.6 [86]

Masahiro Tanaka   RHP

Born: 11/01/88   Age: 32   Bats: R   Throws: R
Height: 6'3"   Weight: 218   Origin: International Free Agent, 2014

YEAR	TEAM	LVL	AGE	W	L	SV	G	GS	IP	H	HR	BB/9	K/9	K	GB%	BABIP
2018	NYY	MLB	29	12	6	0	27	27	156	141	25	2.0	9.2	159	47.5%	.286
2019	NYY	MLB	30	11	9	0	32	31	182	186	28	2.0	7.4	149	47.5%	.293
2020	NYY	MLB	31	3	3	0	10	10	48	48	9	1.5	8.2	44	42.7%	.291
2021 FS	NYY	MLB	32	10	8	0	26	26	150	144	24	2.1	8.2	137	45.3%	.287
2021 DC	NYY	MLB	32	10	9	0	31	31	155	149	25	2.1	8.2	141	45.3%	.287

Comparables: Michael Pineda, James Shields, Ricky Nolasco

When the Yankees inked Tanaka to a seven-year, $155 million pact in January of 2014, the expectation was that he would follow in the footsteps of CC Sabathia, Andy Pettitte and Mike Mussina (among others) and be the next great Yankees ace. Instead, Tanaka has been more of a reliable and dependable mainstay than a frontline arm. This isn't a knock on Tanaka. For a pitcher who eschewed Tommy John surgery way back in 2014 in favor of PRP injections, his results have been quite admirable. Tanaka found some of his lost velocity by throwing his fastball less frequently, and while the formula worked for him for years, his recent launch angle and batted ball trends aren't encouraging. Nevertheless, he fits the part as a solid mid-rotation option, and as of press time, he was in line to cash in as a free agent.

YEAR	TEAM	LVL	AGE	WHIP	ERA	DRA-	WARP	MPH	FB%	WHF	CSP
2018	NYY	MLB	29	1.13	3.75	88	2.5	93.6	31.5%	29.5%	
2019	NYY	MLB	30	1.24	4.45	101	1.6	93.4	32.0%	23.5%	
2020	NYY	MLB	31	1.17	3.56	93	0.6	93.9	32.1%	29.7%	
2021 FS	NYY	MLB	32	1.20	3.75	89	2.3	93.6	31.9%	26.3%	45.6%
2021 DC	NYY	MLB	32	1.20	3.75	89	2.4	93.6	31.9%	26.3%	45.6%

Masahiro Tanaka, continued

Pitch Shape vs LHH

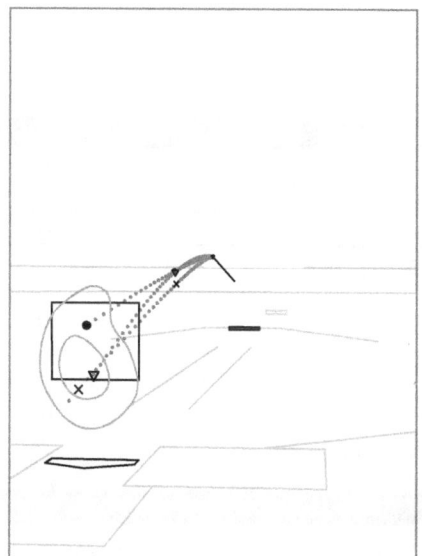

Pitch Shape vs RHH

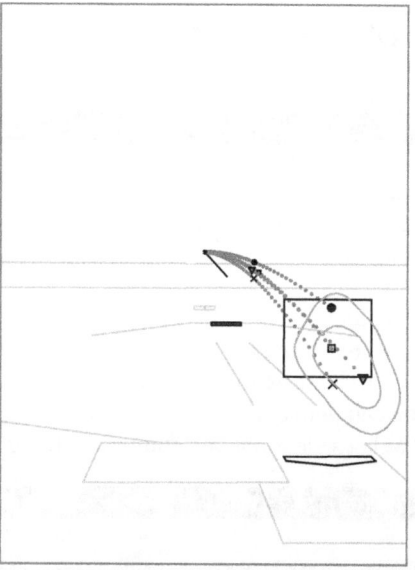

Type	Frequency	Velocity	H Movement	V Movement
● Fastball	24.1%	92.5 [100]	-8.5 [92]	-13.7 [104]
□ Sinker	7.2%	91.7 [96]	-14.6 [89]	-19.8 [103]
✕ Splitter	24.6%	87.2 [109]	-11.5 [87]	-25.2 [114]
▽ Slider	37.5%	84.1 [101]	2.7 [90]	-32.1 [105]
◇ Curveball	5.9%	75.1 [86]	6.4 [95]	-48.2 [100]

New York Yankees 2021

PLAYER COMMENTS WITHOUT GRAPHS

Kevin Alcantara OF
Born: 07/12/02 Age: 18 Bats: R Throws: R
Height: 6'6" Weight: 188 Origin: International Free Agent, 2018

YEAR	TEAM	LVL	AGE	PA	R	2B	3B	HR	RBI	BB	K	SB	CS	AVG/OBP/SLG
2019	YAE	ROK	16	128	19	5	2	1	13	3	27	3	3	.260/.289/.358
2019	DSL NYY	ROK	16	46	7	3	1	0	6	5	9	2	0	.237/.348/.368
2021 FS	NYY	MLB	18	600	40	18	2	7	46	24	207	11	6	.185/.224/.266

Comparables: Isaac Galloway, Rey Fuentes, Xavier Avery

    Alcantara grew up rooting for the Yankees, meaning he can empathize with New York's fan base more than most of his peers. It shouldn't surprise anyone, then, if he's extra motivated to become a starting-caliber outfielder. That way, he can help end the pain and suffering of fans like himself, who have seen the Yankees win only one championship during their lifetimes.

YEAR	TEAM	LVL	AGE	PA	DRC+	BABIP	BRR	FRAA	WARP
2019	YAE	ROK	16	128		.326			
2019	DSL NYY	ROK	16	46		.300			
2021 FS	NYY	MLB	18	600	32	.276	1.2	CF -1	-3.3

Greg Allen LF
Born: 03/15/93 Age: 28 Bats: S Throws: R
Height: 6'0" Weight: 185 Origin: Round 6, 2014 Draft (#188 overall)

YEAR	TEAM	LVL	AGE	PA	R	2B	3B	HR	RBI	BB	K	SB	CS	AVG/OBP/SLG
2018	COL	AAA	25	205	31	13	0	2	14	19	44	12	6	.298/.395/.409
2018	CLE	MLB	25	291	36	11	3	2	20	14	58	21	4	.257/.310/.343
2019	COL	AAA	26	226	37	9	3	5	17	20	44	10	5	.268/.358/.419
2019	CLE	MLB	26	256	30	9	3	4	27	11	53	8	2	.229/.290/.346
2020	SD	MLB	27	4	1	0	0	0	0	2	1	1	0	.000/.750/.000
2020	CLE	MLB	27	28	3	1	0	1	4	1	9	1	0	.160/.214/.320
2021 FS	NYY	MLB	28	600	73	24	2	12	63	42	137	20	7	.241/.322/.368

Comparables: Leonys Martin, Cory Sullivan, Jose Gonzalez

    Allen is what he is at this point: a speedy center fielder incapable of much offensive production. His defense and baserunning are enough to keep him rosterable, but that could change if and when his athleticism slips.

YEAR	TEAM	LVL	AGE	PA	DRC+	BABIP	BRR	FRAA	WARP
2018	COL	AAA	25	205	125	.389	0.3	CF(42): 2.3, LF(5): -0.4, RF(1): 0.5	1.2
2018	CLE	MLB	25	291	78	.320	3.4	CF(78): 2.8, RF(16): -0.4, LF(3): -0.1	0.8
2019	COL	AAA	26	226	95	.322	0.6	CF(26): 1.6, LF(15): 1.4, RF(1): 0.0	0.8
2019	CLE	MLB	26	256	73	.280	0.8	LF(60): 6.0, CF(18): -1.6, RF(13): 0.1	0.4
2020	SD	MLB	27	4	88		0.1	LF(1): -0.0, RF(1): -0.0	0.0
2020	CLE	MLB	27	28	93	.188	0.0	LF(11): 0.3, CF(4): 0.2	0.1
2021 FS	NYY	MLB	28	600	92	.301	1.3	CF 4, LF 2	1.9

Socrates Brito OF
Born: 09/06/92   Age: 28   Bats: L   Throws: L
Height: 6'2"   Weight: 205   Origin: International Free Agent, 2010

YEAR	TEAM	LVL	AGE	PA	R	2B	3B	HR	RBI	BB	K	SB	CS	AVG/OBP/SLG
2018	RNO	AAA	25	478	85	34	5	17	69	44	104	15	4	.318/.383/.540
2018	ARI	MLB	25	44	3	0	0	1	3	3	9	0	1	.175/.227/.250
2019	BUF	AAA	26	428	66	28	7	16	67	29	97	11	7	.282/.328/.510
2019	TOR	MLB	26	43	5	0	1	0	2	4	17	0	0	.077/.163/.128
2021 FS	NYY	MLB	28	600	61	28	7	18	71	37	164	3	2	.240/.293/.414

Comparables: Matt Carson, Alexis Gomez, Cole Garner

If the Platonic ideal prides the purity of an idea over its physical reality, the Socratic Brito ideal prides the promise of tools over their in-game manifestation. An intriguing collection of tools has not yet coalesced into everyday, playable skills, and he's running out of time for that to happen. A rebound project with Toronto, he dropped a rung on the organizational talent ladder in 2019 and left as a free agent, signing with the Pirates. However, he missed summer camp with a positive COVID test, and finally opted out of the season after tragically losing his brother to the virus. He could return to the Pirates, who certainly aren't going anywhere this season, or find another team to take a chance on translating the thought-experiment into reality.

YEAR	TEAM	LVL	AGE	PA	DRC+	BABIP	BRR	FRAA	WARP
2018	RNO	AAA	25	478	136	.384	2.1	RF(66): 5.3, CF(27): 0.3, LF(23): 3.5	3.6
2018	ARI	MLB	25	44	82	.194	0.1	RF(11): -0.1, LF(3): -0.1, CF(1): -0.0	0.0
2019	BUF	AAA	26	428	106	.333	-1.4	LF(44): 1.8, RF(35): 4.8, CF(6): -0.8	1.6
2019	TOR	MLB	26	43	52	.136	0.0	RF(12): -0.8, CF(4): -0.2, LF(1): -0.1	-0.2
2021 FS	NYY	MLB	28	600	85	.311	0.3	RF 4, LF 1	0.9

Jasson Dominguez CF
Born: 02/07/03 Age: 18 Bats: S Throws: R
Height: 5'10" Weight: 190 Origin: International Free Agent, 2019

If you believe the scouting reports, Dominguez is going to be the next great Yankee outfielder as well as one of the greatest hitters ever to play the game. He should cruise into the Hall of Fame, perhaps even before he retires. That last one is a wee bit hyperbolic, but scouts are crushing on the Dominican youngster. In a normal year, there would be at least some looks against live pitching to offer additional information and context regarding Dominguez's ability. Right now, everyone is playing the same guessing game. What we know for sure is that Dominguez is a year older, albeit still only 18, and that the sight of him taking cuts in batting practice can light up a social media feed. While there are many potential outcomes for Dominguez, and they're not all super rosy, there's also virtually no precedent for a 16-year-old signee with such thunderous tools out of the gate. Put a star by his name: either he'll become one, or we'll learn something in the process.

Ezequiel Duran 2B
Born: 05/22/99 Age: 22 Bats: R Throws: R
Height: 5'11" Weight: 185 Origin: International Free Agent, 2017

YEAR	TEAM	LVL	AGE	PA	R	2B	3B	HR	RBI	BB	K	SB	CS	AVG/OBP/SLG
2018	PUL	ROK	19	235	34	8	2	4	20	9	65	7	0	.201/.251/.311
2019	SI	SS	20	277	49	12	4	13	37	25	77	11	4	.256/.329/.496
2021 FS	NYY	MLB	22	600	45	21	3	12	54	27	229	11	5	.185/.229/.301

Comparables: Patrick Wisdom, Darrell Ceciliani, Shane Peterson

Duran hopes to finally make his full-season debut in 2021. He has plenty of raw power, but his build and swing-and-miss issues could eventually stop him in his tracks at the higher levels of the minors.

YEAR	TEAM	LVL	AGE	PA	DRC+	BABIP	BRR	FRAA	WARP
2018	PUL	ROK	19	235		.265			
2019	SI	SS	20	277	160	.314	0.6	2B(57): 7.6	3.0
2021 FS	NYY	MLB	22	600	42	.284	1.5	2B 5, SS 0	-2.0

Thairo Estrada 2B

Born: 02/22/96 Age: 25 Bats: R Throws: R
Height: 5'10" Weight: 185 Origin: International Free Agent, 2012

YEAR	TEAM	LVL	AGE	PA	R	2B	3B	HR	RBI	BB	K	SB	CS	AVG/OBP/SLG
2018	TAM	HI-A	22	47	4	2	0	0	5	0	9	0	0	.222/.234/.267
2018	SWB	AAA	22	34	1	1	0	0	3	0	8	0	0	.152/.176/.182
2019	SWB	AAA	23	259	39	17	2	8	32	14	50	3	1	.266/.313/.452
2019	NYY	MLB	23	69	12	3	0	3	12	3	15	4	0	.250/.294/.438
2020	NYY	MLB	24	52	8	0	0	1	3	1	19	1	0	.167/.231/.229
2021 FS	NYY	MLB	25	600	68	22	1	15	68	30	146	4	3	.241/.291/.371
2021 DC	NYY	MLB	25	62	7	2	0	1	7	3	15	0	0	.241/.291/.371

Comparables: Reid Brignac, Edmundo Sosa, Charlie Culberson

This book is filled with stories of players who could have been helped by a functioning minor-league system, complete with a full slate of games and opportunities to hone their craft and apply the finishing touches in a less-competitive setting. Arguably, there isn't a player who was more screwed by the limitations COVID placed on the game than Estrada. Two years removed from a gunshot wound suffered in a botched robbery attempt, Estrada could have used a healthy consolidation season in the minors as a chance to rediscover his power stroke and cast himself as DJ LeMahieu's heir apparent at the keystone. Instead, 2020 was another lost year for him. He bounced between New York and the alternate site, and he did little with the limited opportunities he received. Estrada isn't old, but the window is narrowing for him to become more than a utility infielder.

YEAR	TEAM	LVL	AGE	PA	DRC+	BABIP	BRR	FRAA	WARP
2018	TAM	HI-A	22	47	52	.270	-0.6	SS(8): -0.2	-0.3
2018	SWB	AAA	22	34	27	.200	-0.3	SS(5): 0.0, 2B(3): 0.9	-0.1
2019	SWB	AAA	23	259	86	.304	-1.1	SS(33): 1.7, 2B(24): -0.9, 3B(2): -0.3	0.5
2019	NYY	MLB	23	69	87	.283	1.0	2B(17): -1.1, SS(9): 0.3, LF(2): -0.1	0.1
2020	NYY	MLB	24	52	61	.250	0.3	2B(20): 0.3, 3B(6): -0.4, SS(3): -0.1	-0.1
2021 FS	NYY	MLB	25	600	79	.299	-0.4	2B -1, 3B -3	-0.4
2021 DC	NYY	MLB	25	62	79	.299	0.0	2B 0, 3B 0	-0.1

New York Yankees 2021

Estevan Florial CF

Born: 11/25/97   Age: 23   Bats: L   Throws: R
Height: 6'1"   Weight: 195   Origin: International Free Agent, 2015

YEAR	TEAM	LVL	AGE	PA	R	2B	3B	HR	RBI	BB	K	SB	CS	AVG/OBP/SLG
2018	TAM	HI-A	20	339	45	16	3	3	27	44	87	11	10	.255/.354/.361
2019	TAM	HI-A	21	301	38	10	3	8	38	24	98	9	5	.237/.297/.383
2020	NYY	MLB	22	3	0	0	0	0	0	0	2	0	0	.333/.333/.333
2021 FS	NYY	MLB	23	600	67	17	3	17	63	46	235	9	5	.202/.269/.343

Comparables: Keon Broxton, Tommy Pham, Daniel Fields

If you're a prospect watcher, it's understandable if you have Florial fatigue. He made his debut on our Top 101 list in 2018 before he was old enough to legally purchase a cocktail, and as tales of his tools and athleticism spread, the blowback was inevitable. Florial has struggled both with making contact and staying healthy, and it's easy to forget that he's just a 23-year-old who did not have an at-bat above A-ball before he made his major-league debut in 2020. It's far too early to put the busted prospect label on him, but he'll need to start developing quickly if he's ever going to make the waiting worth the while.

YEAR	TEAM	LVL	AGE	PA	DRC+	BABIP	BRR	FRAA	WARP
2018	TAM	HI-A	20	339	102	.353	-0.9	CF(59): 1.8, RF(6): -0.2, LF(3): -0.1	0.4
2019	TAM	HI-A	21	301	92	.335	1.0	CF(64): 2.9	1.1
2020	NYY	MLB	22	3	90	1.000		CF(1): -0.1	0.0
2021 FS	NYY	MLB	23	600	63	.317	0.8	CF 5, RF 0	-0.4

Mike Ford 1B

Born: 07/04/92   Age: 29   Bats: L   Throws: R
Height: 6'0"   Weight: 225   Origin: Undrafted Free Agent, 2013

YEAR	TEAM	LVL	AGE	PA	R	2B	3B	HR	RBI	BB	K	SB	CS	AVG/OBP/SLG
2018	SWB	AAA	25	410	48	21	0	15	52	37	70	1	0	.253/.327/.433
2019	SWB	AAA	26	349	59	20	0	23	60	46	55	0	1	.303/.401/.605
2019	NYY	MLB	26	163	30	7	0	12	25	17	28	0	0	.259/.350/.559
2020	NYY	MLB	27	84	5	4	0	2	11	7	16	0	0	.135/.226/.270
2021 FS	NYY	MLB	28	600	83	25	1	29	84	69	124	0	0	.241/.339/.462
2021 DC	NYY	MLB	28	132	18	5	0	6	18	15	27	0	0	.241/.339/.462

Comparables: Jason Giambi, Lyle Overbay, Norm Zauchin

Ford, like the other big-leaguer named Mike who hails from New Jersey, grew up in a suburb that's actually closer to Philadelphia than it is to New York City. Unless Ford is also an Eagles fan (instead of a Giants fan), that's about where the similarities begin and end.

YEAR	TEAM	LVL	AGE	PA	DRC+	BABIP	BRR	FRAA	WARP
2018	SWB	AAA	25	410	114	.275	-0.9	1B(57): -0.2	0.5
2019	SWB	AAA	26	349	141	.300	0.3	1B(44): -3.2, 3B(5): 0.0	1.8
2019	NYY	MLB	26	163	125	.243	-0.6	1B(29): -0.2, P(1): -0.0	0.7
2020	NYY	MLB	27	84	85	.140	-0.2	1B(13): -1.0	-0.1
2021 FS	NYY	MLB	28	600	111	.264	-1.0	1B -2, 3B 0	1.5
2021 DC	NYY	MLB	28	132	111	.264	-0.2	1B 0	0.3

Rosell Herrera OF

Born: 10/16/92 Age: 28 Bats: S Throws: R
Height: 6'3" Weight: 180 Origin:

YEAR	TEAM	LVL	AGE	PA	R	2B	3B	HR	RBI	BB	K	SB	CS	AVG/OBP/SLG
2018	LOU	AAA	25	98	11	8	2	3	11	6	15	2	1	.267/.320/.500
2018	OMA	AAA	25	41	8	3	2	1	5	5	7	4	1	.278/.366/.556
2018	KC	MLB	25	289	25	14	3	1	20	19	52	3	4	.238/.292/.325
2018	CIN	MLB	25	13	0	0	0	0	0	0	5	0	1	.154/.154/.154
2019	NO	AAA	26	180	21	11	1	5	24	14	32	2	1	.309/.367/.479
2019	MIA	MLB	26	119	10	6	0	2	11	11	27	4	1	.200/.288/.314
2021 FS	NYY	MLB	28	600	55	21	2	13	58	48	145	14	5	.217/.285/.336

Comparables: Mark Davidson, Bob Gallagher, Lee Lacy

Maybe it *feels* like longer ago (2020 had a way of aging us), but it hasn't even been a year since Herrera was turning heads in Yankees camp with a 1.044 OPS in his first 27 spring plate appearances. But Herrera's prospects of making the Bombers' squad vasnished along with the spring: He subsequently suffered injuries in both heels, and didn't factor into the team's plans when the season re-started in July. Herrera became a minor-league free agent and signed with the Dragons in December; he'll be the first foreign position player in the CPBL since 2019. His solid offensive performance in the upper minors–119 DRC+ in Triple-A in 2018-2019–and experience at second, third, shortstop and all three outfield positions gives the Dragons some choices in their lineup and around the diamond.

YEAR	TEAM	LVL	AGE	PA	DRC+	BABIP	BRR	FRAA	WARP
2018	LOU	AAA	25	98	123	.292	1.3	3B(7): -0.5, LF(6): -1.1, RF(4): -0.5	0.2
2018	OMA	AAA	25	41	126	.321	0.5	CF(6): 0.4, RF(2): 0.2, LF(1): -0.3	0.3
2018	KC	MLB	25	289	71	.290	1.7	RF(29): -0.4, 2B(17): 0.5, CF(12): -1.3	-0.2
2018	CIN	MLB	25	13	69	.250	-0.1	LF(2): -0.1, 2B(1): -0.1	0.0
2019	NO	AAA	26	180	115	.359	0.5	3B(21): -1.4, LF(12): 0.0, 2B(11): -1.3	0.7
2019	MIA	MLB	26	119	71	.250	0.9	CF(25): -2.0, RF(15): -1.9, LF(13): -0.0	-0.3
2021 FS	NYY	MLB	28	600	72	.271	0.8	RF 0, CF 0	-0.6

Gary Sánchez C

Born: 12/02/92   Age: 28   Bats: R   Throws: R
Height: 6'2"   Weight: 230   Origin: International Free Agent, 2009

YEAR	TEAM	LVL	AGE	PA	R	2B	3B	HR	RBI	BB	K	SB	CS	AVG/OBP/SLG
2018	SWB	AAA	25	28	4	0	0	4	4	0	10	0	0	.179/.179/.607
2018	NYY	MLB	25	374	51	17	0	18	53	46	94	1	0	.186/.291/.406
2019	NYY	MLB	26	446	62	12	1	34	77	40	125	0	1	.232/.316/.525
2020	NYY	MLB	27	178	19	4	0	10	24	18	64	0	0	.147/.253/.365
2021 FS	NYY	MLB	28	600	84	22	0	32	89	55	188	1	1	.220/.306/.449
2021 DC	NYY	MLB	28	465	65	17	0	25	69	43	145	0	1	.220/.306/.449

Comparables: Josmil Pinto, Geovany Soto, Willson Contreras

As a standalone season, you can look at nearly any player's truncated, 60-game sample in 2020 and write it off as a ridiculous fluke, no matter how terrific or awful it was. For Sánchez, it is difficult (if not impossible) to not look at what he did last year as part of a trendline that goes back to 2018.

YEAR	TEAM	P. COUNT	FRM RUNS	BLK RUNS	THRW RUNS	TOT RUNS
2018	NYY	10936	3.3	-4.3	0.2	-0.8
2019	NYY	12715	-5.1	-0.8	-0.2	-6.1
2020	NYY	5546	0.1	-0.4	-0.1	-0.4
2021	NYY	16835	2.6	-3.2	0.5	0.0
2021	NYY	16835	2.6	-5.4	0.5	-2.3

Over the last three years, his .200/.294/.455 slash line ranks 10th among catchers with at least 600 plate appearances, but a big chunk of that production stems from a single season. He was the invisible man in the box last year, with his strikeout rate jumping to a whopping 37 percent thanks to his dwindling contact rate on pitches both inside and outside the zone. (To think, the raw numbers are even a little charitable to Sánchez, as his numbers are aided by an extremely hitter-friendly Yankee Stadium.) The lack of offensive output makes the debates about Sánchez's defense irrelevant. It would have been unthinkable three years ago to think he might not be part of New York's long-term core. Now? It's a serious point to consider.

YEAR	TEAM	LVL	AGE	PA	DRC+	BABIP	BRR	FRAA	WARP
2018	SWB	AAA	25	28	80	.071	0.0	C(5): -0.0	0.0
2018	NYY	MLB	25	374	94	.197	-1.4	C(76): -1.4	1.1
2019	NYY	MLB	26	446	121	.244	-2.5	C(90): -6.3	2.4
2020	NYY	MLB	27	178	84	.159	-0.5	C(41): -0.5	0.0
2021 FS	NYY	MLB	28	600	102	.272	-0.9	C -3	2.3
2021 DC	NYY	MLB	28	465	102	.272	-0.7	C -3	1.7

Mike Tauchman CF

Born: 12/03/90 Age: 30 Bats: L Throws: L
Height: 6'2" Weight: 220 Origin: Round 10, 2013 Draft (#289 overall)

YEAR	TEAM	LVL	AGE	PA	R	2B	3B	HR	RBI	BB	K	SB	CS	AVG/OBP/SLG
2018	ABQ	AAA	27	471	84	26	7	20	81	60	70	12	10	.323/.408/.571
2018	COL	MLB	27	37	5	1	0	0	0	4	15	1	0	.094/.194/.125
2019	SWB	AAA	28	114	22	10	3	2	16	16	16	4	0	.274/.386/.505
2019	NYY	MLB	28	296	46	18	1	13	47	34	71	6	0	.277/.361/.504
2020	NYY	MLB	29	111	18	6	0	0	14	14	26	6	0	.242/.342/.305
2021 FS	NYY	MLB	30	600	72	21	2	17	67	59	147	7	3	.224/.307/.369
2021 DC	NYY	MLB	30	130	15	4	0	3	14	12	32	1	1	.224/.307/.369

Comparables: Mike Young, Jason Michaels, Geoff Jenkins

One of the most difficult things about baseball, besides the obvious idea that you must see the ball and hit the ball, is getting into and maintaining the rhythm required to perform the feat. Tauchman quickly morphed from the happy-go-lucky story of 2019 into a frustrating player who wasn't able to squeeze enough playing time out of a crowded Yankees outfield to ever get it going. The power that suddenly appeared in 2019 disappeared just as quickly last season, and while the perennial injuries to Aaron Judge and Giancarlo Stanton opened the door for Tauchman, his subpar performance and the emergence of Clint Frazier slammed it shut. One poor season (and a truncated one at that) isn't the death knell for his career, but Tauchman will soon cross into his 30s and will need to rediscover whatever magic he had in '19 if he's going to be anything more than a fourth outfielder.

YEAR	TEAM	LVL	AGE	PA	DRC+	BABIP	BRR	FRAA	WARP
2018	ABQ	AAA	27	471	146	.345	3.5	CF(65): 4.2, LF(30): 6.1, RF(15): 1.7	4.8
2018	COL	MLB	27	37	52	.176	0.1	CF(5): -0.1, LF(3): -0.9, RF(1): -0.0	-0.2
2019	SWB	AAA	28	114	115	.308	1.2	CF(15): 0.4, LF(7): 1.4, RF(6): 0.7	0.8
2019	NYY	MLB	28	296	112	.333	2.4	LF(59): 5.3, RF(19): -0.5, CF(14): -0.8	1.9
2020	NYY	MLB	29	111	93	.329	0.0	LF(20): 2.0, RF(19): 0.8, CF(5): 0.0	0.4
2021 FS	NYY	MLB	30	600	83	.279	0.1	RF 2, LF 4	1.0
2021 DC	NYY	MLB	30	130	83	.279	0.0	RF 0, LF 1	0.2

Anthony Volpe 2B

Born: 04/28/01   Age: 20   Bats: R   Throws: R
Height: 5'11"   Weight: 180   Origin: Round 1, 2019 Draft (#30 overall)

YEAR	TEAM	LVL	AGE	PA	R	2B	3B	HR	RBI	BB	K	SB	CS	AVG/OBP/SLG
2019	PUL	ROK+	18	150	19	7	2	2	11	23	38	6	1	.215/.349/.355
2021 FS	NYY	MLB	20	600	44	18	2	8	47	40	220	9	3	.176/.239/.268

Most scouting reports on Volpe refer to him as "steady" and "reliable," rather than spectacular. While there's something to be said for a high floor (perceived or otherwise), that's often just a fancy way of saying he has a low ceiling.

YEAR	TEAM	LVL	AGE	PA	DRC+	BABIP	BRR	FRAA	WARP
2019	PUL	ROK+	18	150		.289			
2021 FS	NYY	MLB	20	600	40	.273	0.7		-2.8

Tyler Wade SS

Born: 11/23/94   Age: 26   Bats: L   Throws: R
Height: 6'1"   Weight: 188   Origin: Round 4, 2013 Draft (#134 overall)

YEAR	TEAM	LVL	AGE	PA	R	2B	3B	HR	RBI	BB	K	SB	CS	AVG/OBP/SLG
2018	SWB	AAA	23	408	46	18	4	4	27	37	82	11	8	.255/.328/.360
2018	NYY	MLB	23	70	8	4	0	1	5	4	23	1	0	.167/.214/.273
2019	SWB	AAA	24	335	51	19	4	4	38	23	76	13	5	.296/.352/.425
2019	NYY	MLB	24	108	16	3	1	2	11	11	28	7	0	.245/.330/.362
2020	NYY	MLB	25	105	19	3	0	3	10	12	22	4	1	.170/.288/.307
2021 FS	NYY	MLB	26	600	69	25	2	13	60	53	152	11	4	.233/.310/.364
2021 DC	NYY	MLB	26	186	21	7	0	4	18	16	47	3	1	.233/.310/.364

Comparables: Cesar Crespo, Mark Bellhorn, Damian Jackson

It's understandable if you don't want to dive into a comment about Wade, a glove-first, bat-second utility player who, using replacement-level value as a fathometer, has been underwater since joining the Yankees in 2017. He spent the entire year with the big club, but that had more to do with the team's multiple injuries and the absence of a Triple-A team than it did with anything he accomplished. His ability to play any position on the diamond and speed is nice, though he doesn't offer enough with the bat to be more than a reserve. That's fine and all, you just can't say that his major-league tenure has gone swimmingly.

YEAR	TEAM	LVL	AGE	PA	DRC+	BABIP	BRR	FRAA	WARP
2018	SWB	AAA	23	408	97	.318	-2.1	SS(51): -0.2, LF(12): 2.1, 2B(10): 1.7	1.1
2018	NYY	MLB	23	70	55	.238	1.7	2B(26): -0.6, RF(5): -0.1, SS(2): 0.0	-0.1
2019	SWB	AAA	24	335	92	.381	1.6	SS(43): 2.6, 2B(28): 0.7, 3B(4): 0.6	1.4
2019	NYY	MLB	24	108	72	.328	0.5	2B(18): 1.8, LF(14): 0.1, 3B(5): -0.5	0.1
2020	NYY	MLB	25	105	91	.188	0.0	2B(31): 2.0, SS(22): -3.2	0.1
2021 FS	NYY	MLB	26	600	83	.301	0.5	SS -1, 2B 3	0.7
2021 DC	NYY	MLB	26	186	83	.301	0.2	SS 0, 2B 1	0.3

Austin Wells   C
Born: 07/12/99   Age: 21   Bats: L   Throws: R
Height: 6'2"   Weight: 220   Origin: Round 1, 2020 Draft (#28 overall)

With the exception of Aaron Judge, the first round of the draft has been an exercise in failure and futility for the Yankees over the past decade-plus; the last non-Judge player to sign with the Yanks and make any sort of impact in the majors was Ian Kennedy in 2006. Drafting a catcher probably isn't the best way to break the streak, but the Yankees couldn't pass on Wells and his offensive promise. There's a real chance he's going to have to move out from behind the plate in due time, perhaps before he catches a big-league pitch, yet the hope is that he'll have the stick to stand in left field or possibly first base. Hope hasn't gotten the Yankees far in recent drafts, but what's another penny in the well when you can have a hitter like Wells for pennies?

Albert Abreu   RHP

Born: 09/26/95   Age: 25   Bats: R   Throws: R
Height: 6'2"   Weight: 190   Origin: International Free Agent, 2013

YEAR	TEAM	LVL	AGE	W	L	SV	G	GS	IP	H	HR	BB/9	K/9	K	GB%	BABIP
2018	TAM	HI-A	22	4	3	0	13	13	62^2	54	9	4.2	9.3	65	43.4%	.278
2019	TRN	AA	23	5	8	0	23	20	96^2	103	9	4.9	8.5	91	41.2%	.339
2020	NYY	MLB	24	0	1	0	2	0	1^1	4	1	13.5	13.5	2	33.3%	.600
2021 FS	NYY	MLB	25	2	3	0	57	0	50	50	9	6.0	8.4	46	39.9%	.299
2021 DC	NYY	MLB	25	2	2	0	45	0	22	22	4	6.0	8.4	20	39.9%	.299

Comparables: Hector Perez, Jordan Yamamoto, Keury Mella

If you're a fan of power arms, Abreu is your guy. His fastball–an upper 90s offering with lots of spin and late life–is so electric that the mound should be surrounded with a fence that has one of those "DANGER: HIGH VOLTAGE" signs attached to it during his half-innings. He also sports a quality power curve he can command and mixes in a slider and change when needed. The catch is Abreu can't stay healthy, to the extent that there are legitimate concerns he'll never be able to get a full season of reps as a starting pitcher. He has the stuff to be an elite reliever, but he's running the risk of becoming just another face in a loaded and crowded Yankees bullpen.

YEAR	TEAM	LVL	AGE	WHIP	ERA	DRA-	WARP	MPH	FB%	WHF	CSP
2018	TAM	HI-A	22	1.32	4.16	81	1.0				
2019	TRN	AA	23	1.61	4.28	139	-2.2				
2020	NYY	MLB	24	4.50	20.25	112	0.0	98.5	51.2%	33.3%	
2021 FS	NYY	MLB	25	1.68	6.04	125	-0.5	98.5	51.2%	33.3%	40.1%
2021 DC	NYY	MLB	25	1.68	6.04	125	-0.2	98.5	51.2%	33.3%	40.1%

Matt Bowman   RHP

Born: 05/31/91   Age: 30   Bats: R   Throws: R
Height: 6'0"   Weight: 185   Origin: Round 13, 2012 Draft (#410 overall)

YEAR	TEAM	LVL	AGE	W	L	SV	G	GS	IP	H	HR	BB/9	K/9	K	GB%	BABIP
2018	MEM	AAA	27	0	1	1	18	0	23	23	2	3.1	11.7	30	54.8%	.350
2018	STL	MLB	27	0	2	0	22	0	23	29	4	4.3	10.2	26	46.5%	.385
2019	LOU	AAA	28	1	1	4	29	0	39	28	1	4.2	8.1	35	55.3%	.265
2019	CIN	MLB	28	2	0	0	27	0	32	27	2	3.7	7.0	25	54.5%	.258
2021 FS	NYY	MLB	30	2	2	0	57	0	50	46	5	3.2	8.1	45	52.3%	.287

Comparables: Luis Cessa, Justin Grimm, Ramon E Ramirez

A veteran low-leverage reliever, Bowman hurt his elbow in summer camp and underwent Tommy John surgery in September; he's likely out until the 2022 season, but that didn't stop the Yankees from signing him to a two-year minor-league pact in December.

YEAR	TEAM	LVL	AGE	WHIP	ERA	DRA-	WARP	MPH	FB%	WHF	CSP
2018	MEM	AAA	27	1.35	4.30	41	0.8				
2018	STL	MLB	27	1.74	6.26	123	-0.2	93.8	60.1%	20.5%	
2019	LOU	AAA	28	1.18	2.08	77	0.9				
2019	CIN	MLB	28	1.25	3.66	100	0.2	94.5	72.9%	19.1%	
2021 FS	NYY	MLB	30	1.28	3.65	85	0.7	94.3	69.2%	19.5%	46.3%

Jhoulys Chacín   RHP

Born: 01/07/88   Age: 33   Bats: R   Throws: R
Height: 6'3"   Weight: 215   Origin: International Free Agent, 2004

YEAR	TEAM	LVL	AGE	W	L	SV	G	GS	IP	H	HR	BB/9	K/9	K	GB%	BABIP
2018	MIL	MLB	30	15	8	0	35	35	192²	153	18	3.3	7.3	156	41.2%	.254
2019	BOS	MLB	31	0	2	0	6	5	14²	16	6	4.3	12.9	21	38.5%	.303
2019	MIL	MLB	31	3	10	0	19	19	88²	99	19	4.0	8.1	80	36.6%	.312
2020	ATL	MLB	32	1	0	0	2	0	5	6	1	5.4	5.4	3	16.7%	.294
2021 FS	NYY	MLB	33	2	3	0	57	0	50	51	10	3.9	8.0	44	39.0%	.293

Comparables: Edwin Jackson, Trevor Cahill, Kyle Gibson

One of the many disposable veterans signed as depth for Atlanta's pitching staff, Chacín lived up to that tag as well as anyone, throwing five unremarkable innings in relief before getting the boot.

YEAR	TEAM	LVL	AGE	WHIP	ERA	DRA-	WARP	MPH	FB%	WHF	CSP
2018	MIL	MLB	30	1.16	3.50	100	1.8	92.2	48.1%	21.4%	
2019	BOS	MLB	31	1.57	7.36	83	0.3	91.8	44.3%	24.6%	
2019	MIL	MLB	31	1.56	5.79	142	-1.2	91.8	43.5%	20.1%	
2020	ATL	MLB	32	1.80	7.20	128	0.0	92.4	42.4%	0.0%	
2021 FS	NYY	MLB	33	1.46	5.17	114	-0.1	92.0	45.5%	20.2%	48.0%

Nestor Cortes LHP

Born: 12/10/94 Age: 26 Bats: R Throws: L
Height: 5'11" Weight: 210 Origin: Round 36, 2013 Draft (#1094 overall)

YEAR	TEAM	LVL	AGE	W	L	SV	G	GS	IP	H	HR	BB/9	K/9	K	GB%	BABIP
2018	SWB	AAA	23	6	6	0	23	18	111^2	95	13	3.0	7.7	96	33.3%	.264
2018	BAL	MLB	23	0	0	0	4	0	4^2	10	2	7.7	5.8	3	47.4%	.471
2019	SWB	AAA	24	2	2	0	7	6	39^2	29	3	2.5	9.5	42	35.0%	.263
2019	NYY	MLB	24	5	1	0	33	1	66^2	75	16	3.8	9.3	69	34.5%	.321
2020	SEA	MLB	25	0	1	0	5	1	7^2	12	6	7.0	9.4	8	35.7%	.286
2021 FS	NYY	MLB	26	2	2	0	57	0	50	47	8	3.4	8.6	47	35.5%	.282

Comparables: Ryan Helsley, Jake Newberry, Alex Reyes

One thing we've discovered over the years is that ERA is a *terrible* metric to measure pitching quality. It's fair to assume Cortes is very grateful we figured that out. Unfortunately, the only number that can help him stay employed is 570,500, his near-minimum salary. It probably won't be enough.

YEAR	TEAM	LVL	AGE	WHIP	ERA	DRA-	WARP	MPH	FB%	WHF	CSP
2018	SWB	AAA	23	1.18	3.71	112	-0.1				
2018	BAL	MLB	23	3.00	7.71	96	0.0	90.1	62.0%	24.4%	
2019	SWB	AAA	24	1.01	3.86	53	1.6				
2019	NYY	MLB	24	1.54	5.67	132	-0.8	91.5	51.8%	25.9%	
2020	SEA	MLB	25	2.35	15.26	172	-0.2	90.3	40.6%	20.3%	
2021 FS	NYY	MLB	26	1.32	4.38	99	0.3	91.3	50.3%	24.9%	47.7%

Domingo Germán   RHP

Born: 08/04/92   Age: 28   Bats: R   Throws: R
Height: 6'2"   Weight: 181   Origin: International Free Agent, 2009

YEAR	TEAM	LVL	AGE	W	L	SV	G	GS	IP	H	HR	BB/9	K/9	K	GB%	BABIP
2018	TAM	HI-A	25	0	0	0	2	2	6	3	0	3.0	12.0	8	15.4%	.231
2018	NYY	MLB	25	2	6	0	21	14	85²	81	15	3.5	10.7	102	39.1%	.300
2019	NYY	MLB	26	18	4	0	27	24	143	125	30	2.5	9.6	153	37.5%	.260
2021 FS	NYY	MLB	28	9	8	0	26	26	150	135	25	3.3	9.7	161	38.7%	.288
2021 DC	NYY	MLB	28	6	5	0	19	16	95	86	16	3.3	9.7	102	38.7%	.288

Comparables: Joe Ross, Joe Musgrove, Nick Pivetta

Germán's year was far more notable for what he didn't do than what he did. In February, he escaped a dune buggy accident in his native Dominican Republic unscathed. In July, he then posted a salty comment on Instagram saying he was "done with baseball" before backtracking almost immediately thereafter. Germán's season was already shortened pre-COVID due to having to serve the remainder of an 81-game suspension under MLB-MLBPA's Joint Domestic Violence Policy, and when the season was cut to 60 games, any chance of him playing baseball disappeared along with it. The Yankees could have used Germán in the postseason, but announced they wouldn't due to a lack of preparation time. He still has plenty of potential but has a great deal of work to do both on and, perhaps more importantly, off the field if he hopes to make it back to the majors.

YEAR	TEAM	LVL	AGE	WHIP	ERA	DRA-	WARP	MPH	FB%	WHF	CSP
2018	TAM	HI-A	25	0.83	0.00	38	0.2				
2018	NYY	MLB	25	1.33	5.57	97	0.9	96.3	46.9%	32.6%	
2019	NYY	MLB	26	1.15	4.03	87	2.3	95.4	44.9%	28.3%	
2021 FS	NYY	MLB	28	1.27	3.97	92	2.1	95.7	45.4%	29.4%	47.2%
2021 DC	NYY	MLB	28	1.27	3.97	92	1.3	95.7	45.4%	29.4%	47.2%

Luis Gil RHP

Born: 06/03/98   Age: 23   Bats: R   Throws: R
Height: 6'2"   Weight: 185   Origin: International Free Agent, 2015

YEAR	TEAM	LVL	AGE	W	L	SV	G	GS	IP	H	HR	BB/9	K/9	K	GB%	BABIP
2018	PUL	ROK	20	2	1	0	10	10	39^1	21	1	5.7	13.3	58	34.2%	.256
2018	SI	SS	20	0	2	0	2	2	6^2	11	1	8.1	13.5	10	39.1%	.455
2019	CSC	LO-A	21	4	5	0	17	17	83	60	1	4.2	12.1	112	47.2%	.311
2019	TAM	HI-A	21	1	0	0	3	3	13	11	0	5.5	7.6	11	40.5%	.297
2021 FS	NYY	MLB	23	2	3	0	57	0	50	44	8	7.1	9.8	54	38.7%	.284

Comparables: Domingo Germán, Albert Abreu, Gregory Infante

Appearances can be deceiving. In Gil's case, the ease and effortlessness of his delivery make it seem like he should have plenty of command and control at his disposal. Alas, this isn't the case at all, and his command veers anywhere between "average" and "nonexistent." Gil's upper-90s fastball and slurvy curve are both quality offerings, but a combination of his inconsistent command and his lack of a third pitch make it more likely that he's going to be a future bullpen arm than a rotation mainstay.

YEAR	TEAM	LVL	AGE	WHIP	ERA	DRA-	WARP	MPH	FB%	WHF	CSP
2018	PUL	ROK	20	1.17	1.37						
2018	SI	SS	20	2.55	5.40	300	-0.9				
2019	CSC	LO-A	21	1.19	2.39	80	1.3				
2019	TAM	HI-A	21	1.46	4.85	115	-0.1				
2021 FS	NYY	MLB	23	1.68	5.47	116	-0.2				

Ben Heller RHP

Born: 08/05/91   Age: 29   Bats: R   Throws: R
Height: 6'3"   Weight: 210   Origin: Round 22, 2013 Draft (#651 overall)

YEAR	TEAM	LVL	AGE	W	L	SV	G	GS	IP	H	HR	BB/9	K/9	K	GB%	BABIP
2019	SWB	AAA	27	0	0	1	9	4	11	5	0	2.5	10.6	13	54.5%	.227
2019	NYY	MLB	27	0	0	0	6	0	7^1	6	1	3.7	11.0	9	43.8%	.357
2020	NYY	MLB	28	0	0	0	6	0	6	5	2	3.0	9.0	6	29.4%	.200
2021 FS	NYY	MLB	29	2	2	0	57	0	50	43	7	4.5	10.5	58	41.8%	.295

Comparables: Shawn Armstrong, Juan Minaya, Santiago Casilla

It took five years and four seasons of sporadic innings for Heller to exhaust his rookie eligibility, a product of both the team's vaunted bullpen depth and an unfortunately-timed UCL tear. As a result, it remains unclear whether he can replicate his minor-league dominance in the majors.

YEAR	TEAM	LVL	AGE	WHIP	ERA	DRA-	WARP	MPH	FB%	WHF	CSP
2019	SWB	AAA	27	0.73	0.82	36	0.5				
2019	NYY	MLB	27	1.23	1.23	103	0.0	94.7	49.0%	36.8%	
2020	NYY	MLB	28	1.17	3.00	106	0.0	94.9	51.4%	26.5%	
2021 FS	NYY	MLB	29	1.37	4.25	96	0.3	94.8	50.5%	30.4%	42.2%

Corey Kluber   RHP
Born: 04/10/86   Age: 35   Bats: R   Throws: R
Height: 6'4"   Weight: 215   Origin: Round 4, 2007 Draft (#134 overall)

YEAR	TEAM	LVL	AGE	W	L	SV	G	GS	IP	H	HR	BB/9	K/9	K	GB%	BABIP
2018	CLE	MLB	32	20	7	0	33	33	215	179	25	1.4	9.3	222	44.5%	.277
2019	CLE	MLB	33	2	3	0	7	7	35²	44	4	3.8	9.6	38	39.3%	.374
2020	TEX	MLB	34	0	0	0	1	1	1	0	0	9.0	9.0	1	0.0%	.000
2021 FS	NYY	MLB	35	10	7	0	26	26	150	138	23	2.7	9.0	149	42.3%	.288
2021 DC	NYY	MLB	35	9	7	0	24	24	138.3	128	21	2.7	9.0	138	42.3%	.288

Comparables: Max Scherzer, Zack Greinke, Johnny Cueto

    The Texas Rangers were founded in 1823. Not the baseball team, but the law enforcement unit. For more than a century the organization was responsible for apprehending outlaws across the nation, achieving national notoriety and public adoration alike, blending a no-nonsense attitude with unquestionable results. Kluber was a natural fit for the brand. When the two-time Cy Young winner joined the Rangers (the baseball team this time) last December, there were some injury concerns. Kluber pitched one competitive inning in 2020, and the team declined his $18 million option, making him a free agent. All told, he burned bright and reached the pinnacle of his profession twice, even starting three of the seven World Series games in 2016. There's something poetic about the aging gunslinger reaching deep down for one last ride, one last pitch. Whether or not it's that time for Kluber, like his Ranger namesakes, his Texas-sized presence is certainly receding.

YEAR	TEAM	LVL	AGE	WHIP	ERA	DRA-	WARP	MPH	FB%	WHF	CSP
2018	CLE	MLB	32	0.99	2.89	63	6.1	93.8	41.6%	27.1%	
2019	CLE	MLB	33	1.65	5.80	127	-0.2	93.5	39.8%	28.5%	
2020	TEX	MLB	34	1.00	0.00	107	0.0	93.0	50.0%	12.5%	
2021 FS	NYY	MLB	35	1.22	3.63	86	2.6	93.7	41.2%	27.3%	45.5%
2021 DC	NYY	MLB	35	1.22	3.63	86	2.4	93.7	41.2%	27.3%	45.5%

Luis Medina   RHP

Born: 05/03/99   Age: 22   Bats: R   Throws: R
Height: 6'1"   Weight: 175   Origin: International Free Agent, 2015

YEAR	TEAM	LVL	AGE	W	L	SV	G	GS	IP	H	HR	BB/9	K/9	K	GB%	BABIP
2018	PUL	ROK	19	1	3	0	12	12	36	32	3	11.5	11.8	47	42.7%	.337
2019	CSC	LO-A	20	1	8	0	20	20	93	86	9	6.5	11.1	115	43.6%	.344
2019	TAM	HI-A	20	0	0	0	2	2	10^2	7	0	2.5	10.1	12	67.9%	.250
2021 FS	NYY	MLB	22	2	3	0	57	0	50	47	9	8.8	9.3	51	43.0%	.288

Comparables: Huascar Ynoa, Beau Burrows, Jefry Rodriguez

The Yankees seem to pluck pitchers who throw super hard and have a subpar command profile out of thin air. Medina is potentially the most promising of New York's endless cavalcade of arms of this ilk. His secondary pitches quietly improved, pushing him past the limitations of two-pitch bullpen arm while his arm action, athleticism and physicality suggest there is more growth to come. Medina wasn't able to convince the Yankees brass to overlook his lack of experience in the high minors and push him to the majors for a 2020 relief debut, but when and if the minors resume play it's likely that his raw stuff will put him on the fast track to the Bronx.

YEAR	TEAM	LVL	AGE	WHIP	ERA	DRA-	WARP	MPH	FB%	WHF	CSP
2018	PUL	ROK	19	2.17	6.25						
2019	CSC	LO-A	20	1.65	6.00	145	-2.1				
2019	TAM	HI-A	20	0.94	0.84	72	0.2				
2021 FS	NYY	MLB	22	1.92	6.78	137	-0.8				

James Paxton LHP

Born: 11/06/88 Age: 32 Bats: L Throws: L
Height: 6'4" Weight: 227 Origin: Round 4, 2010 Draft (#132 overall)

YEAR	TEAM	LVL	AGE	W	L	SV	G	GS	IP	H	HR	BB/9	K/9	K	GB%	BABIP
2018	SEA	MLB	29	11	6	0	28	28	160^1	134	23	2.4	11.7	208	39.8%	.301
2019	NYY	MLB	30	15	6	0	29	29	150^2	138	23	3.3	11.1	186	39.0%	.315
2020	NYY	MLB	31	1	1	0	5	5	20^1	23	4	3.1	11.5	26	32.1%	.365
2021 FS	NYY	MLB	32	10	7	0	26	26	150	134	23	3.0	10.5	175	38.9%	.297
2021 DC	NYY	MLB	32	7	6	0	21	21	111.3	100	17	3.0	10.5	130	38.9%	.297

Comparables: Stephen Strasburg, Matt Harvey, Dallas Keuchel

Paxton's 2020 got off to an inauspicious start even before pitchers and catchers reported, as he required spinal surgery in early February with an estimated recovery time of three-to-four months. Paxton appeared to benefit from the delayed start, but even though he started the newly abbreviated season on time, he looked off his game. His velocity was several miles per hour lower than it had been in 2019, and after five starts, he was shut down for good, this time with a flexor strain. There's no denying that he's an above-average starter when healthy; the question is if he can be relied upon to throw more than 120-140 frames as he heads deeper into his 30s.

YEAR	TEAM	LVL	AGE	WHIP	ERA	DRA-	WARP	MPH	FB%	WHF	CSP
2018	SEA	MLB	29	1.10	3.76	59	4.9	97.7	63.6%	30.1%	
2019	NYY	MLB	30	1.28	3.82	85	2.6	97.6	59.9%	30.7%	
2020	NYY	MLB	31	1.48	6.64	103	0.2	93.8	56.7%	28.4%	
2021 FS	NYY	MLB	32	1.22	3.69	86	2.7	97.2	60.6%	30.3%	48.8%
2021 DC	NYY	MLB	32	1.22	3.69	86	2.0	97.2	60.6%	30.3%	48.8%

Clarke Schmidt RHP

Born: 02/20/96 Age: 25 Bats: R Throws: R
Height: 6'1" Weight: 200 Origin: Round 1, 2017 Draft (#16 overall)

YEAR	TEAM	LVL	AGE	W	L	SV	G	GS	IP	H	HR	BB/9	K/9	K	GB%	BABIP
2018	YAE	ROK	22	0	2	0	3	2	7²	8	1	2.3	14.1	12	50.0%	.412
2018	YAW	ROK	22	0	0	0	3	3	7¹	4	0	2.5	9.8	8	68.8%	.250
2018	SI	SS	22	0	1	0	2	2	8¹	4	0	2.2	10.8	10	36.8%	.211
2019	YAE	ROK	23	0	0	0	3	3	8¹	6	1	3.2	15.1	14	56.2%	.333
2019	TAM	HI-A	23	4	5	0	13	12	63¹	59	2	3.4	9.8	69	54.6%	.333
2019	TRN	AA	23	2	0	0	3	3	19	14	1	0.5	9.0	19	45.1%	.260
2020	NYY	MLB	24	0	1	0	3	1	6¹	7	0	7.1	9.9	7	42.1%	.368
2021 FS	NYY	MLB	25	9	9	0	26	26	150	143	25	4.0	8.9	148	41.3%	.292
2021 DC	NYY	MLB	25	4	3	0	19	6	54.3	52	9	4.0	8.9	53	41.3%	.292

Comparables: Dillon Peters, Jonathan Loaisiga, Elieser Hernandez

Schmidt made his debut in 2020, becoming the first person from Acworth, Georgia to reach the majors. Acworth has a rich and storied history but is more recently known as the city where several scenes from the 2011 version of *Footloose* were filmed. Schmidt's dream isn't to break free of a strict minister who won't allow dancing in his small town, but to break into the Yankees' rotation. And he isn't being held back from that dream by a man of the cloth, but rather, by the need for more reps, something he was unable to get last year thanks to shuttering of the minors. We'll see if the Yankees let Schmidt cut loose and kick off his Sunday shoes, or if they'll be Reverend Shaw Moore to his Ren McCormack and keep him burning, yearning and punching his card in the minors for another year.

YEAR	TEAM	LVL	AGE	WHIP	ERA	DRA-	WARP	MPH	FB%	WHF	CSP
2018	YAE	ROK	22	1.30	7.04						
2018	YAW	ROK	22	0.82	1.23						
2018	SI	SS	22	0.72	1.08	245	-0.6				
2019	YAE	ROK	23	1.08	3.24						
2019	TAM	HI-A	23	1.31	3.84	84	0.7				
2019	TRN	AA	23	0.79	2.37	79	0.3				
2020	NYY	MLB	24	1.89	7.11	90	0.1	96.4	54.0%	21.8%	
2021 FS	NYY	MLB	25	1.41	4.65	105	1.0	96.4	54.0%	21.8%	48.4%
2021 DC	NYY	MLB	25	1.41	4.65	105	0.3	96.4	54.0%	21.8%	48.4%

Luis Severino RHP

Born: 02/20/94 Age: 27 Bats: R Throws: R
Height: 6'2" Weight: 218 Origin: International Free Agent, 2011

YEAR	TEAM	LVL	AGE	W	L	SV	G	GS	IP	H	HR	BB/9	K/9	K	GB%	BABIP
2018	NYY	MLB	24	19	8	0	32	32	191^1	173	19	2.2	10.3	220	41.5%	.315
2019	NYY	MLB	25	1	1	0	3	3	12	6	0	4.5	12.8	17	37.5%	.250
2021 FS	NYY	MLB	27	10	7	0	26	26	150	131	21	2.7	10.5	174	41.7%	.296
2021 DC	NYY	MLB	27	5	3	0	16	14	74.3	65	10	2.7	10.5	86	41.7%	.296

Comparables: Germán Márquez, Aaron Nola, Yovani Gallardo

Despite the 1.50 ERA and the absurd 35 percent strikeout rate in three starts to close out 2019, there were warning signs about Severino's health that, in retrospect, made the forearm soreness he suffered from in the postseason and the subsequent Tommy John surgery he underwent in spring more predictable. His velocity was down to its pre-2018 levels, his command looked shaky and perhaps worst of all, he was more tentative about using his devastating slider. Severino's rehab is going well, but he still isn't expected back in pinstripes until June or July of 2021. He has thrown a combined 20 1/3 innings in the regular season and postseason in the last two years, so it's to be determined what he'll have to offer once he returns.

YEAR	TEAM	LVL	AGE	WHIP	ERA	DRA-	WARP	MPH	FB%	WHF	CSP
2018	NYY	MLB	24	1.14	3.39	62	5.6	99.4	50.5%	26.9%	
2019	NYY	MLB	25	1.00	1.50	83	0.2	98.0	56.6%	27.5%	
2021 FS	NYY	MLB	27	1.18	3.32	81	3.1	99.2	51.2%	26.9%	50.7%
2021 DC	NYY	MLB	27	1.18	3.32	81	1.5	99.2	51.2%	26.9%	50.7%

Jameson Taillon RHP

Born: 11/18/91 Age: 29 Bats: R Throws: R
Height: 6'5" Weight: 230 Origin: Round 1, 2010 Draft (#2 overall)

YEAR	TEAM	LVL	AGE	W	L	SV	G	GS	IP	H	HR	BB/9	K/9	K	GB%	BABIP
2018	PIT	MLB	26	14	11	0	33	33	198	186	20	2.1	8.4	184	46.0%	.301
2019	PIT	MLB	27	2	3	0	7	7	37^1	34	4	1.9	7.2	30	48.3%	.263
2021 FS	NYY	MLB	29	10	7	0	26	26	150	140	19	2.5	8.5	141	47.0%	.291
2021 DC	NYY	MLB	29	7	5	0	16	19	103	96	13	2.5	8.5	97	47.0%	.291

Comparables: Gerrit Cole, Joe Musgrove, Michael Wacha

Now a two-time Tommy John veteran as well as a cancer survivor, Taillon's so tough, anchors have tattoos of him. The former second-overall pick knows the odds of pitchers returning successfully from a second TJ surgery are against him, but he's buoyed by a positive attitude and survivor's mindset, fueled by the extensive time he's spent giving back in charitable endeavors around Pittsburgh. He's also optimistic about significant changes he's made in his mechanics (shortening his arm path) and delivery (using his legs more) which he says have his elbow feeling better than ever, and has also adjusted his training and recovery schedule to focus on long-term arm health. The odds might not be favorable, but Taillon makes it very hard to bet against him. Who would want to, anyway?

YEAR	TEAM	LVL	AGE	WHIP	ERA	DRA-	WARP	MPH	FB%	WHF	CSP
2018	PIT	MLB	26	1.18	3.18	76	4.2	96.7	57.3%	24.1%	
2019	PIT	MLB	27	1.12	4.10	76	0.8	96.4	47.2%	24.2%	
2021 FS	NYY	MLB	29	1.22	3.47	84	2.8	96.6	54.5%	24.2%	48.5%
2021 DC	NYY	MLB	29	1.22	3.47	84	1.9	96.6	54.5%	24.2%	48.5%

Yankees Prospects

The State of the System:
A deep, talent-rich org with immediate help for 2021 and beyond, finally things are looking up for the New York Yankees.

The Top Ten:

─────── ★ ★ ★ *2021 Top 101 Prospect* **#17** ★ ★ ★ ───────

1
Deivi García   RHP   OFP: 70   ETA: Debuted in 2020
Born: 05/19/99   Age: 22   Bats: R   Throws: R   Height: 5'9"   Weight: 163
Origin: International Free Agent, 2015

The Report: Yes, García is deceptive, but don't let that term fool you—he has four average-or-better pitches and misses a ton of bats. His fastball is anywhere from 90-96 mph, and while it doesn't have particularly notable spin rates, it fools hitters; we think this is a combination of good shape and a difficult to pick up release point that comes from deception in his delivery and his height. His curveball is just a straight plus-plus breaking ball, a classic high-spin, two-plane bender that will serve as his out pitch and plays very well off his fastball. García also has a changeup that functions as an average arm-side offering and a slider which he developed over the course of 2019 that has flashed higher. Despite the deception, his delivery is low-effort, and he's run huge strikeout rates all over the minors even though he's always been one of the youngest players at his level.

Development Track: The Yankees called García up at the end of August. He flashed glimpses of frontline brilliance while making six league-average starts down the stretch just a few months after his 21st birthday. His command was significantly sharper than he'd shown in the minors; he was able to spot all of his pitches effectively around the zone.

Variance: Medium. We know the stuff can get past major-league hitters already, and the command profile looked a lot more consistent than it did previously. He's still a pitcher with an oddball profile, but that's about all that's working against him here.

Mark Barry's Fantasy Take: García was only okay in his first stint against big-league hitters, but let's not overthink this. Unless the Yankees go on a major spending spree between now and Opening Day, García should begin the season as the number-two starter in the Bronx. We don't know what kind of workload he'll be able to withstand early, but I'd expect plenty of strikeouts and wins in the meantime.

★ ★ ★ *2021 Top 101 Prospect* **#59** ★ ★ ★

2 Jasson Dominguez CF   OFP: 70   ETA: 2024 or 2025
Born: 02/07/03   Age: 18   Bats: S   Throws: R   Height: 5'10"   Weight: 190
Origin: International Free Agent, 2019

The Report / Development Track: In last year's blurb we noted that we had very limited information with which to pin down a ranking for Dominguez. Almost nothing has changed in that regard. The demographics which suggest he's a top prospect (signing bonus, teenage showcase and tricky league reports) also would have applied to Kevin Maitan a few years ago. The reports were good mind you, a potential five-tool outfielder with light tower power. Dominguez was briefly stateside for spring training pre-shutdown, but was not invited to the alternate site, and the Yankees did not run domestic instructs in the Fall. Occasional Instagram video emerged of the 17-year-old—now built like a short-yardage running back that Gene Stallings would have recruited for his early 90s Alabama teams—taking massive home run cuts in some sort of live batting practice. We can safely conclude the raw power is still present, but beyond that we really have no idea what kind of prospect Dominguez is at this point.

Variance: Extreme. If I could go higher than extreme I would.

Mark Barry's Fantasy Take: Dominguez is a prime mystery box guy. He could be anything. He could be two tickets to a comedy club, or he could be a boat. Unfortunately he's being priced as a boat. He could absolutely be worth it, and judging on his Instagram feed, he could be quite exciting. It's just that his stock is already sky-high, so if you didn't already get in, you're likely to be priced out. I think Dominguez is a top-20ish dynasty prospect, and he's absolutely the type of player I'd be likely to flip for a veteran.

★ ★ ★ *2021 Top 101 Prospect* **#96** ★ ★ ★

3 Clarke Schmidt RHP   OFP: 60   ETA: Debuted in 2020
Born: 02/20/96   Age: 25   Bats: R   Throws: R   Height: 6'1"   Weight: 200
Origin: Round 1, 2017 Draft (#16 overall)

The Report: Schmidt's calling card is an elite two-plane breaking ball. It has slider velocity, sitting in the mid-80s, with curveball shape. Schmidt calls it a curveball. Whatever the nomenclature, the spin rates on it are top-of-the-league (3085 average rpm in 2020) and it's a visually stunning pitch. If he can command it, it has a chance to be one of the best breaking balls in the majors. Schmidt also has both four-seam and two-seam fastball varieties in the mid-90s, with the two-seamers generally looking the best to us and the four-seamers often showing significant cut.

Changeup development, command, and durability are all significant drags on Schmidt's profile. His change was a show-me pitch in the minors in 2019, and that continued in his brief 2020 MLB stint; he threw it less than 9 percent of the time. His command has come and gone. And Schmidt just hasn't pitched a whole lot as a pro, as the Yankees brought him back very slowly and very carefully from pre-draft Tommy John surgery, limiting his workload into the 2019 season.

Development Track: A few days after they called on García, the Yankees brought up Schmidt. He didn't pitch much, and he was wild and relatively ineffective, but his curveball spin rates remained obscene. Before things got shut down, Schmidt was one of the most impressive pitchers in the Grapefruit League, and we suspect he'd have gotten much more of an opportunity in a normal season.

Variance: High. Schmidt has a scant professional track record through his first four seasons, and the command and changeup would carry significant bullpen risk on their own.

Mark Barry's Fantasy Take: We've seen fewer than 120 professional innings from Schmidt, and he has been relatively steady, if not dominant. I'm a little worried about volume for Schmidt, but he has displayed a knack for missing bats at every stop, and should continue to do so in the Bronx if he can stay on the bump. His situation and upside keeps him above streamer status for me.

4   Luis Gil   RHP   OFP: 60   ETA: Late 2022/2023
Born: 06/03/98   Age: 23   Bats: R   Throws: R   Height: 6'2"   Weight: 185
Origin: International Free Agent, 2015

The Report: Out of the pitchers in the Yankees org who haven't debuted in the majors, Gil possibly has the highest ceiling. Owning the best fastball in the system, Gil creates downhill plane along with electrifying, late life on a pitch that can comfortably sit in the upper-90s. The heater is a true swing-and-miss offering already. During 2020, Gil worked on honing his strike-throwing ability, which was a concern after 2019. He also worked on getting his slurvy breaking ball to resemble more of a slider, adding a few ticks to it as well. Gil's low-90s changeup, similar to a power sinker, is also a potential plus offering.

Development Track: Gil has yet to eclipse 100 innings in his minor league career, and with no games during 2020, he may not be able to pass that mark in 2021 either. But right now, developing his breaking ball is more important. How this pitch develops will determine how fast he moves.

Variance: High. Although the fastball is currently plus, tinkering with the arsenal means there is still much that is unknown. Until we can see the secondary improvements play out in live games, and Gil has more successful innings above Low-A, reliever risk is still present—albeit with high-leverage potential.

Mark Barry's Fantasy Take: The lack of true secondary offerings keeps me off Gil Island for the time being, as I'm having a hard time shaking the reliever risk. He could be a very good reliever, mind you, but that's not something you should go out looking for. I'm passing for now, but I'll monitor the progress.

5. Luis Medina   RHP   OFP: 60   ETA: Late 2022/2023
Born: 05/03/99   Age: 22   Bats: R   Throws: R   Height: 6'1"   Weight: 175
Origin: International Free Agent, 2015

The Report: Medina's big turnaround happened late in the 2019 season. The key change for the right-hander's surge began when he started using his curveball more than half the time, helping his plus-plus fastball, which has touched as high as 102, play up even more. But it wasn't just the pitch mix that helped Medina. Gradually, he began throwing more strikes, cutting his walk rate down. In winter ball, that trend has continued. Over 11 2/3 innings in Liga de Baseball Professional Roberto Clemente, Medina has fanned 25 against just four walks. There are no obvious mechanical culprits for his previous wildness, so improving his strike rate even more with the curveball has been a point of emphasis throughout the year. With the curveball and fastball getting most of the attention, it is easy to forget about the 90 mph changeup. Even though it will mostly be used against lefties, it is a solid offering to round out a menacing arsenal.

Development Track: The 2020 season was lined up for Medina to make a significant jump in innings, after throwing around 100 the previous two years. He did get innings at the alternate site and in Puerto Rico, but the lost frames surely will push his timeline back. How much will depend on how normal the minors are in 2021 and if his dominant performances from High-A continues. Medina will only be entering his age-22 season so don't expect the Yankees to push him too fast.

Variance: High. Although the variance has shrunk over the last year-plus, the track record isn't quite there yet to alleviate all concerns. Medina has certainly raised the floor, but there's still a ways to go for the young hurler.

Mark Barry's Fantasy Take: Of the Bronx Luises, I actually prefer Medina to Gil for dynasty purposes. I have more confidence in Medina's ability to start long-term, and his arsenal is already fairly well developed. He'll need some polishing this season, but if he continues on this development path, it isn't difficult to imagine some SP2-SP3 seasons from Medina. I'm not sure that's enough to crack the top-100, but he'd be in that next group of 50 names for me.

6. Estevan Florial   CF   OFP: 55   ETA: Debuted in 2020
Born: 11/25/97   Age: 23   Bats: L   Throws: R   Height: 6'1"   Weight: 195
Origin: International Free Agent, 2015

The Report: Three years ago, we ranked Florial as the No. 26 prospect in baseball. He'd shown thunderous bat speed from the left side with big power potential, and we were pretty optimistic about him finding a good plate approach and ending up with an above-average hit tool. He'd shown up in the Double-A Eastern League playoffs as a teenager after seemingly mastering both full-season A-ball levels, and there was about as much scout buzz as any player in baseball.

Just about nothing has gone right for Florial since. He battled recurring hamate and wrist problems during 2018 and 2019, hitting poorly at return engagements in High-A when on the field. The pitch recognition and plate approach went backwards, and we haven't seen the potentially above-average hit tool in a few years either. The bat speed and raw power are still there, but he hasn't been able to get to it in games.

Development Track: The Yankees called Florial up as a spare outfielder when needed; you can probably tell throughout this chapter that they weren't shy about calling prospects up. He started a game in center and looked overmatched twice against Michael Wacha before roping a single off Walker Lockett. He did go to the Dominican this winter and got some at-bats in during the LIDOM season, playing well there, but a mostly-lost season for a player who needed to get things back on track is never good.

Variance: High. Florial really needed a healthy consolidation season, and it's hard to tell where he's at lacking much new information.

Mark Barry's Fantasy Take: Florial's prospect status joins the long list of New York falls from grace that includes former mayors, former shortstops (before a return to grace?), and the Knicks. Admittedly that's a bit harsh, but since peaking at number 26 on the 2018 101, Florial has done little else to instill confidence that he can restore the buzz. I hope he has a moment, but I think the consistency(or lack thereof) those moments will keep the ceiling low.

7 Anthony Volpe   2B   OFP: 55   ETA: 2023
Born: 04/28/01   Age: 20   Bats: R   Throws: R   Height: 5'11"   Weight: 180
Origin: Round 1, 2019 Draft (#30 overall)

The Report: The less-heralded prep teammate of likely top 2021 selection Jack Leiter, Volpe was the one who actually went in the first round in 2019. He's a well-rounded infield prospect, and I liked him a good deal in high school. Volpe has above-average bat speed, and his quick hands lend well to a positive future hit tool outcome, although he's had so few reps against professional hitting that it's hard to be aggressive until we see him more as a pro. His swing plane has not shown optimization for power yet, and whether or not he can develop significant game power is an open question. Defensively, he has a shot to remain at shortstop, with second and third as potential fallback spots. With his lack of experience, there's a bit of a mystery box flair here, but as of before he was shut down in 2019, there was not an obvious carrying tool present, even if there were several that could get there.

Development Track: The Yankees were conservative with alternate site invites, bypassing most of their far-away prospect crop, and then they didn't hold domestic fall instructs at all. So there's not much official action for us to update going on here, although we've heard that Volpe is training well in the tri-state area.

Variance: High. His entire pro experience is 34 games in the Appy League.

Mark Barry's Fantasy Take: Volpe is fine. Maybe he's even a little better than that. But the ability to "stick at short" isn't as much of a selling point as it once was, with the current batch of MLBers at the six providing real, top-of-draft output. If you want to tab Volpe as a future second baseman, and roll the dice in leagues with at least 200 prospects, that sounds about right.

8. Kevin Alcantara OF OFP: 55 ETA: Late 2023/2024
Born: 07/12/02 Age: 18 Bats: R Throws: R Height: 6'6" Weight: 188
Origin: International Free Agent, 2018

The Report: Alcantara showed his upside in flashes after coming stateside as a 16-year-old in 2019. In the GCL, he chased out of the zone regularly and overall showed an inconsistent swing. However across 2020, Alcantara began controlling the zone better while cutting down on the big movements in his swing. Mechanically, he's now more repeatable and plays much better against all pitch types. There is a chance Alcantara will hit for both power and average, as his plus bat speed will help both tools grow. The long and slender 6-foot-6 outfielder also added much needed strength to his frame, lifting his power tool floor without taking away speed yet, but that will remain a concern down the road. Defensively, the arm is plus and Alcantara has the potential to be a center fielder in the long term. As he physically develops, however, he may get pushed to right field.

Development Track: With Alcantara purportedly making big strides this year, some expect him to move quickly over the next season or two as he gets his feet under him stateside. But regardless, he still has lots of work to do in front of him, with playing close to a full season near the top of the to-do list.

Variance: Very high. The possible mix of five above-average to plus tools make Alcantara an enticing prospect. But with little to no track record and still only 18 years old, he makes for a better dream than a sure-fire bet at this point.

Mark Barry's Fantasy Take: As dynasty managers, we're always on the lookout for the next, shiny thing. Estevan Florial isn't cool anymore. You know what's cool? Kevin Alcantara. The latter offers five above-average tools and hasn't yet trailed off in production, or had the bloom fall off his rose. As such, he's a top 100-125 guy in dynasty circles, almost exclusively based on speculative value.

9. Ezequiel Duran 2B   OFP: 55   ETA: 2023
Born: 05/22/99   Age: 22   Bats: R   Throws: R   Height: 5'11"   Weight: 185
Origin: International Free Agent, 2017

The Report: Duran profiles as a power-hitting second baseman who had already figured out how to get much of his plus raw power into games as a teenager. He led the Penn League in home runs in 2019, rarely having to sell out to yank the ball over the fence, while just as comfortably driving the ball into the gaps. The power will eventually play line-to-line if his approach improves. The approach was lacking in short-season, as he didn't always see spin well, and would hunt fastballs out of the zone. Nothing that looked unfixable, however.

On the dirt, Duran projects as a plus defender at second. While the straight-line speed and range are merely average, he's an instinctual defender who shows excellent actions and a strong, accurate arm for the right side of the infield.

Development Track: Duran showed approach gains especially against breaking balls, while continuing to post major-league quality exit velocities. It was a lost year of game reps, though, and it's difficult to gauge exactly where he is now until we see him in Tampa or Hudson Valley in 2021.

Variance: High. This was a tough lost year for the variance profile, given the hit tool concerns and lack of games above short-season.

Mark Barry's Fantasy Take: I read reports like this on Duran and get irrationally excited before seeing Ben's Jonathan Schoop comp from last year and oh right, that's where I've seen this before. I'm considerably less interested in a guy who strikes out almost 30 percent of the time in Low-A, even if said guy has the tools to be a high-power, good defender at the keystone.

10. Austin Wells C   OFP: 50   ETA: 2023
Born: 07/12/99   Age: 21   Bats: L   Throws: R   Height: 6'2"   Weight: 220
Origin: Round 1, 2020 Draft (#28 overall)

The Report: Sometimes you're meant to be a Yankee. Originally drafted by the pinstripes in the 35th round out of high school and then again in the first round this past draft, Wells' reputation as an offensive-minded player carried over to college at the University of Arizona—a notoriously hitter-friendly home park. An impressive summer at the Cape dispelled the notion he was a park-created slugger, but a major question remains: where does he end up defensively? He's spent a majority of his college time at catcher, with starts mixed-in at first base and in the outfield. His receiving skills are so-so at best and his arm is below-average. With such an advanced stick, it may push his inevitable transition from out behind home plate even more quickly.

Development Track: The Yankees have been known to push defensively-challenged catchers before (see: Sánchez, Gary). Wells projects as a complete hitter with contact and power to all fields, so of course that type of player would be of supreme value if he could stick at the position. We'll know within the first week of the (assumed) minor league season what Yankees player development has in store.

Variance: Medium. There is little worry he'll be able to hit his way up the system. He's more athletic than a traditional plodding DH, so you'd like to find a home for him somewhere on the field to keep him in the lineup every day.

Mark Barry's Fantasy Take: Personally I think the Yankees should just have an entire roster of catchers that can't really catch. That should be their thing. Honestly, I might have wells as the third-best dynasty prospect in this system. I think he can hit, and the only question is where he'll play defensively, which pretty much only matters if he sticks behind the plate.

The Prospects You Meet Outside The Top Ten

Top Ten prospects in a shallower system

Josh Breaux   C   Born: 10/07/97   Age: 23   Bats: R   Throws: R   Height: 6'1"   Weight: 220   Origin: Round 2, 2018 Draft (#61 overall)

After playing in only 51 games in 2019, one might think losing the 2020 season would be a huge detriment for Breaux. From all indications, however, it had the opposite effect, as he has reportedly made some of the biggest strides in the org this year anyway. The big-framed catcher's throwing elbow has fully recovered from his 2019 injury, and did not affect his development this year. But his plus-plus arm strength was never the main concern behind the plate. Going forward the glove may not be a problem either with Breaux showing improvements across the board defensively. At the dish in 2019, he swatted an impressive 13 homers in his abbreviated Sally League campaign—albeit with swing-and-miss issues as well. He spent 2020 fine-tuning his swing mechanics to try and cut down on inconsistencies and whiffs, which has so far been positive. A big 2021 campaign from Breaux—assuming a somewhat normal season—would not be surprising.

Roansy Contreras   RHP   Born: 11/07/99   Age: 21   Bats: R   Throws: R   Height: 6'0"   Weight: 175   Origin: International Free Agent, 2016

Compared to the other young Dominican starting pitching prospects in the Yankees org—Gil, Medina, and Alexander Vizcaino—Contreras is far from the flashiest, but he has shown plenty of upside in his own right. In 2019, he excelled in the Sally while throwing plenty of strikes with a three-pitch arsenal: fastball, curveball and changeup. Contreras worked on his curveball this past year to improve consistency and shape, a pitch he needs to stick as a starter. Adding strength and gaining more body control will be top priorities as well.

Prospects to dream on a little

Alexander Vizcaino   RHP   Born: 05/22/97   Age: 24   Bats: R   Throws: R   Height: 6'2"   Weight: 160   Origin: International Free Agent, 2016

Sporting one of the best changeups in the org, Vizcaino made significant improvements during the 2019 season, especially throwing strikes. But one area still in need of development is his fastball, as his mid-to-upper-90s offering got hit harder than you'd think it would in A-ball given the velocity. Avoiding the hard contact on the four-seamer became the main area of focus for the 23-year-old during the pandemic-ridden year. Like Contreras, adding strength to the frame to help with his body control has been a point of emphasis. For what it's worth, the slider will be fine.

Alexander Vargas   SS   Born: 10/29/01   Age: 19   Bats: S   Throws: R   Height: 5'11"   Weight: 148   Origin: International Free Agent, 2018

With a plus speed/glove combo at shortstop, Vargas' ceiling hinges on his hit tool development, due to the lack of projectable power. In 2019 he showed a good swing and approach from both sides while taking his walks. The main concern for Vargas was lack of strength, which he worked on adding in 2020. He fits the mold of the other shortstops in the org: high defensive floor with limited offensive upside.

Maikol Escotto   SS   Born: 06/04/02   Age: 19   Bats: R   Throws: R   Height: 5'11"   Weight: 180   Origin: International Free Agent, 2018

Although he hasn't made his stateside debut yet, Escotto is someone worth keeping an eye on. During the 2019 Dominican Summer League, the now 18-year-old slashed .315/.429/.552 with 13 stolen bases, 11 doubles and eight homers over 45 games. Escotto can reach triple-digit exit velos using a smooth right-handed swing with plus bat speed and plays both middle infield positions as well as third base.

Oswald Peraza   SS   Born: 06/15/00   Age: 21   Bats: R   Throws: R   Height: 6'0"   Weight: 176   Origin: International Free Agent, 2016

A bit of a surprise 40-man add given his total lack of experience above A-ball, Peraza's potential plus shortstop glove and speed might have made him a target in the Rule 5. He was overmatched at the plate at times in the South Atlantic League, but there's some whippy bat speed and above-average raw that could come out with more game experience.

MLB arms, but probably relievers

Albert Abreu   RHP   Born: 09/26/95   Age: 25   Bats: R   Throws: R   Height: 6'2"   Weight: 190   Origin: International Free Agent, 2013

We ranked Abreu third on this list last year, because both Jeffrey and I saw starts where he was still projecting as a mid-rotation starter with electric stuff. He was pretty similar to Medina and Gil as prospects. Where they still have time, Abreu is now 25, and instead of making a quick major-league impact the command was abysmal and his stuff was down in his limited major-league time; he didn't exactly get sterling reviews from the alternate site either, although he's pitched okay in LIDOM this winter (albeit with too many walks, a running theme). Abreu can still hit the upper-90s and there's been a plus breaker projection down there for a half-decade, but he's quickly running out of time to develop the command and sequencing to start, and there were no brilliant outings to ensorcel us for another year in 2020.

T.J. Sikkema   LHP   Born: 07/25/98   Age: 22   Bats: L   Throws: L   Height: 6'0"   Weight: 221   Origin: Round 1, 2019 Draft (#38 overall)

Sikkema is a polished lefty crossfire guy that can hit 95 and show you two different breaking ball looks. 95-and-a-slider-and-a-curve isn't as pithy, but the end result is likely the same—a good major leaguer reliever. Of course this is also the exact type of arm the Yankees are good at coaching up into an OFP 55 in the Florida State League, but that didn't happen this year for obvious reasons.

Miguel Yajure   RHP   Born: 05/01/98   Age: 23   Bats: R   Throws: R   Height: 6'1"   Weight: 175   Origin: International Free Agent, 2015

Unlike Abreu, Yajure looked pretty good in his limited major-league time. He's also not strictly or even necessarily probably a reliever—he's a four-pitch righty with an advanced changeup and good feel for pitching—but he fits in this oeuvre even if it isn't strictly speaking the right category. Yajure has been a scout favorite for years and projects as a fourth starter, but that's the result from after he got his developmental boosts.

You always need catching

Anthony Seigler   C   Born: 06/20/99   Age: 22   Bats: S   Throws: S   Height: 6'0"   Weight: 200   Origin: Round 1, 2018 Draft (#23 overall)

For the third year in-a-row, the 2018 first rounder lost out on crucial game development. In 2019, Seigler only managed to play in 30 games because of two injuries. Defensively, there isn't much worry. He's seen as a plus defender behind the dish, throwing arm especially, with his dexterity helping him make pitch framing improvements. At the plate, however, question marks remain. There really is no projectable power, so the upside offensively will be his ability to get on base and draw walks, which Seigler has shown to be an average strength thus far.

Top Talents 25 and Under (as of 4/1/2021):

1. Gleyber Torres, SS/2B
2. Deivi García, RHP
3. Jasson Dominguez, OF
4. Clarke Schmidt, RHP
5. Luis Gil, RHP
6. Luis Medina, RHP
7. Estevan Florial, OF
8. Anthony Volpe, SS
9. Kevin Alcantara, OF
10. Ezequiel Duran, 2B

Gleyber Torres went from hitting 38 homers in 2019 to 3 in 2020. Sure, the pandemic skews that number, but he still went from slugging .535 to .368, and he also struggled badly at shortstop after previously playing a fine second base. The outcome moving forward is probably going to lie in the middle of all this; he's projected for plus game power since he was a prospect, but 2019 suggested he might contend for home run titles. If only he could play all his games against 2019 Orioles pitching...

I thought about putting Michael King, long a personal favorite, on this list. But he's pretty similar to Yajure, except without the plus change; neither has had much MLB success yet and neither has much more than a fourth starter upside.

Part 3: Featured Articles

Yankees All-Time Top 10 Players

by Steven Goldman

POSITION PLAYERS

BILL DICKEY, C (1928–1943, 1945–1945)

The most frequently repeated story about Dickey comes in slightly different forms, but the basic version is this: During World War II an obscure former player, Joe Gantenbein, approached Dickey on the street. "I bet you don't remember me," Gantenbein says. "I don't recall your name," Dickey responds, "but we used to pitch you high and inside." Dickey kept his eye on the bottom line, a quality that not only made him a standout player but kept him in the game as a coach. With a little help from old Yankee Stadium and the era in which he played (not to mention great ability), Dickey remains one of the best-hitting catchers of all time. Because he played during an era when most catchers were given substantial time off (in his case including a long suspension for breaking another player's jaw after a play at the plate in 1932) most of his individual seasons don't look as good as that of his peers on a volume basis, but his .313/.382/.486 career rates sustained over 1800 games is competitive with every backstop except Mike Piazza.

YOGI BERRA, C (1946–1963)

Yankees owner/executive Larry MacPhail signed Berra sight-unseen, then pretended to be appalled when Berra's World War II service ended and he first reported to Yankee Stadium. MacPhail had forgotten that one of the best aspects of baseball is that it admits more than the classic physical type—you can be successful if you're a skyscraper-like Aaron Judge or hydrant-ish like Berra. Manager Casey Stengel once said that the secret to his Yankees success was, "I never play a game without my man." He was referring to Berra, and he was getting at two of Berra's chief skills, both unusual for a catcher: He was durable and consistent, putting up great numbers almost every year while catching a number of games that would have broken most backstops. He won three MVP awards and finished second in two other seasons, and in that the press rated him correctly: He wasn't always the league's most-productive player, but he was the most indispensable.

LOU GEHRIG, 1B (1923–1939)

So good he shattered the taboo against winning the MVP award twice—it was one-and-done until Gehrig picked up the 1936 award to go with the 1927 honors. A first-generation American who picked up his relentless work ethic from his mother, Gehrig remains overqualified for baseball's Hall of Fame. He was an exemplar of the way Americans like to see themselves: Rising above his parents' station, intensely committed to his job, self-sacrificing, and excellent despite not being the world's most naturally gifted athlete—he had the muscular frame, the speed, the eye, but lacked great agility, and might have been pushed to designated hitter today. He fought literally until he could fight no more and then declared himself the luckiest man on the face of the Earth. He was anti-fascist, too. Remember him not as a man for baseball season, but for all seasons.

WILLIE RANDOLPH, 2B (1976–1992)

Criminally underrated throughout his career, in part because injuries and a low-scoring era kept him from amassing larger numbers. Had he been able to turn his four seasons of 91-99 runs scored into 100s some of the deceptive blandness of his numbers might have been erased. As it was he was an excellent fielder—not notably rangy but excellent on the double play despite a parade of weak partners at short after the decline of Bucky Dent—who reliably got on base at a high rate due to a selective approach at the plate. Far more than the acquisition of Reggie Jackson, it was the outright theft of a December 1975 trade with the Pirates that brought Randolph home to New York that kicked off the mini-dynasty of 1976-1981.

ALEX RODRIGUEZ, 3B (2004–2013, 2015–2016)

Only five Yankees have hit 50 home runs in a season: Babe Ruth (four times), Mickey Mantle (twice), Roger Maris, A-Rod, and Aaron Judge. Note the prevalence of outfielders: Until Rodriguez arrived, third base was not a position where the Yankees had many consistently outstanding offensive players. Many of them, including the future Hall of Famers Home Run Baker, Joe Sewell, and Wade Boggs were good but not necessarily at their best in pinstripes. Graig Nettles had power and was in the same class as Brooks Robinson and Mike Schmidt with the glove but struggled to hit left-handers—it was his glove that made him an everyday player. Though controversial and often unpopular, Rodriguez was the only third baseman in franchise history to qualify as a true year-in, year-out MVP-level player.

DEREK JETER, SS (1995-2014)

The Yankees had gone their whole history without having a shortstop who could consistently hit at a high level before Jeter came along. In the shorter term, they had gone without a quality shortstop at all after the decline of Bucky Dent, a significant factor holding the team back during their long 1982-1994 absence from the postseason. Jeter ended all of that. His limited range to his left was his only significant flaw, but a missed grounder is a single; Jeter had a career .377 on-base percentage and 4,921 total bases, more than any career shortstop except Cal Ripken Jr. The Yankees came out way ahead on the exchange.

BABE RUTH, OF (1920-1934)

Ruth had significant structural advantages over the modern player, among them watered-down competition due to segregation. And yet, how this affected his production is beside the point. First, it was prodigious regardless. Second, it was pioneering, showing the possibilities of what could be done with the lively ball provided one discarded the contact-oriented orthodoxy of the times. More important than both was the way his outsized personality matched his outsized production and interacted with the rise of mass media to capture the affection of a nation. In this way he helped change baseball from pastime to big business. Even when he was at his lowest and meanest, such as in 1922, he was still larger than life, captivating, fun. Even if he didn't really call his shot, he called his shot—it's the myth that matters.

JOE DIMAGGIO, OF (1936-1951)

He remains a mystery, a ballplayer of the highest precision who did not let many people inside. For those interested in nature-vs.-nurture arguments you have the disparate and uneven talents of the three DiMaggio brothers, one of whom hit for a high average and power and never stuck out, another who hit for power but was the most strikeout-prone hitter of his era, while the third was a singles hitter. All three were first-generation Americans who adopted the national game and excelled, leaving behind their father's life as a San Francisco fisherman. Once asked why he went all out in a meaningless, sparsely-attended game, he said that there might be someone there who had never seen him before. When he felt that he was no longer up to giving that unknown fan his best, he walked away. Pride is rated a sin, but in DiMaggio's case it motivated him to give his best and take only what he had earned with that effort.

MICKEY MANTLE, OF (1951-1968)

Mantle's in-career struggles with injuries and great expectations and the post-career revelation of his struggles with addiction have given him a frisson of potential squandered. Even he thought that was the case, and it was tremendously unfair. We'll never know if a more focused and mature Mantle, not to mention a luckier Mantle who had avoided some of his flukier injuries would have been better than he was. What we can say for certain is that the three MVP awards he won represented an insufficient appreciation of how good he was. An argument can be made that, in addition to the 1956, 1957, and 1962 awards he could have received it in 1955, 1958, 1959, and 1961—at minimum.

BERNIE WILLIAMS, OF (1991–2006)

It was so easy to focus on what he couldn't do. He was a switch-hitter who sometimes struggled from his dominant side. He was fast but was a poor baserunner. He played center field but couldn't throw and tended to play too shallow so catchable balls went over his head. He took long walks between pitches. Yet he was a tremendous player who could hit for average and power and excelled at getting on base with a career .381 on-base percentage. He hit over .300 in eight consecutive seasons. Along with Jorge Posada and Derek Jeter, he gave the Yankees strength up the middle which was almost impossible for the competition to match.

PITCHERS

BOB SHAWKEY, RHP (1915–1927)

Discovered by Connie Mack, "Sailor Bob" was sold to the Yankees as part of his mid-1910s teardown. A curveballer who seems to have been able to pitch through sketchy mechanics that would have shredded a lesser arm, he was already a good pitcher when he reached New York but kicked things into a higher gear with four 20-win seasons, an ERA title, and the durability to make frequent "stopper" appearances in relief—he twice led the American League in saves (retroactively figured). He had the bad timing to become manager in the aftermath of Miller Huggins' death; too many raucous ex-teammates looked on him as a pal rather than an authority figure and he was thrown over when Joe McCarthy became available. He forever remains the first pitcher to start a game at Yankee Stadium (original flavor).

WAITE HOYT, RHP (1921–1930)

"The Brooklyn Schoolboy" was only a Yankee for part of his 21-year major league career, but it was the phase he cherished most—he never got over his joy at being part of the 1927 Yankees and a teammate of Babe Ruth's. As long as Hoyt's career was—and he was in the majors for 21 years—his career is also a testament to how managers' profligate pitcher usage could damage arms. Hoyt averaged 253 innings a year from ages 21 through 28. Though he had some good years in his 30s, possibly after adding a slider to his repertoire, he was never as good—or as durable—as he had been. Fortunately, almost all of his World Series experience came while he was still at his peak, and he owns a sparkling 1.83 ERA in 83.2 postseason innings.

LEFTY GOMEZ, LHP (1930–1942)

"Goofy" is almost as well remembered for his quips as his pitching excellence. A hard thrower who thrice led the American League in strikeouts, Gomez saw out the transition from the Yankees of Ruth and Gehrig to that of DiMaggio, Tommy Henrich, and Charlie Keller. Gomez could be a bit of a ham and some of his humor seems a little overbearing, like the comedy relief in a war picture. At his best, though, he reminded people of the way the game could back even the best into a no-win situation. Facing Jimmie Foxx on one occasion he shook off every sign Bill Dickey gave him. Dickey jogged out to the mound to ask what he did want to throw? Nothing, Gomez said. He was just hoping that if they waited long enough Foxx would get bored and go away. Foxx hit .338/.467/.738 off of Gomez for his career, so he had a point... Gomez's best seasons, 1934 (26-5, league-leading 2.33 ERA) and 1937 (21-11, another league-leading 2.33 ERA), remain among the best in team history. Among post-Deadball era pitchers only Ron Guidry exceeded him.

RED RUFFING, RHP (1930–1942, 1945–1946)

A hard thrower and an early adoptee of the slider, Ruffing teaches us that no pitcher is an island. Reaching the majors with a miserable Red Sox team, he was coached poorly and supported miserably, twice losing over 20 games. Dumped on the Yankees for journeyman outfielder Cedric Durst and $50,000, he blossomed when given a manager who was an ex-pitcher (Bob Shawkey) and knew how to improve his mechanics as well as superior offensive and defensive players around him. Contrary to myth, Ruffing didn't emerge as an ace all at once—it was a few years before he achieved the consistency that allowed four consecutive 20-win seasons from 1936 through 1939. One of the best-hitting pitchers of all time, he hit over .300 in seven full seasons (here defined as 100 plate appearances).

WHITEY FORD, LHP (1950, 1953–1967)

Like his friend Mickey Mantle, there is a strange, retroactively applied myth to Ford that counts his career as something of a disappointment because Casey Stengel rationed his usage until 1960. Given that Stengel's successor stopped rationing him—in his first four years under Ralph Houk, Ford pitched almost two-thirds as many innings as he had pitched in the previous eight years under Stengel—and blew his arm out within four years, this calls for wishful thinking that ignores whatever Stengel knew about Ford's condition that caused him to use him as he did (arm problems were not unknown to Ford even then) and the reality of pitcher fragility, which is universal. In other words, in an alternate universe there's a version of Ford who compiled higher counting totals earlier but also got hurt sooner and perhaps came back after throwing junk, something he largely managed to avoid in this reality. We always want the perfect present even presented with a wealth of gifts.

MEL STOTTLEMYRE, RHP (1964–1974)

Sinker-slider control pitcher who came along at exactly the wrong time, Stottlemyre made the majors just in time to experience the last dynastic postseason before the team's long wilderness years. An additional misfortune was his pitching for Ralph Houk, a poor handler of pitchers who was one of the slowest hooks in the majors throughout his career. Resultantly, Stottlemyre averaged 272 innings a season until his arm gave out. Although he missed out on the team's revival as a result, one hopes his five World Series rings as a pitching coach were some consolation.

RON GUIDRY, LHP (1975–1988)

"Louisiana Lightning" was almost thrown away a couple of times. Billy Martin didn't believe in him at first. Bill Veeck asked for him in the Bucky Dent trade and George Steinbrenner was amenable until Gabe Paul objected (future Cy Young winner LaMarr Hoyt went to the White Sox instead). Showing forbearance with a young pitcher for the last time until Andy Pettitte came along, Guidry was allowed to establish himself. The reward was Guidry's 1978, one of the best single-season performances of the postwar era. Guidry's mechanics were heavy on arm action without much leg drive and he was of small stature; that the Yankees asked him to carry 250 innings a year was unwise. And yet the results were so often excellent it's easy to see why they failed to restrain themselves.

ANDY PETTITTE, LHP (1995–2003, 2007–2010, 2012–2013)

Only intermittently an ace-level pitcher (see 1997 and, between Yankees stints, 2005) but almost always solidly above average, Pettitte might have been as famous for his pickoff move as his stuff on the mound. Thanks to his entire career taking place on good teams in the era of multi-round playoffs, he was also better known for postseason performances (19-11, 3.81 ERA in 44 starts) than he was for his regular-season pitching. Aside from his two peak seasons he was one of the most consistent pitchers of all time, and that was true up to the moment he chose to walk away for the last time. Reliability over almost 20 years is as much a skill as striking out 300 batters a year for five.

MARIANO RIVERA, RHP (1995–2013)

Modern closers have a soft job; managers use them to the saves rule instead of deploying them in the most critical situations. What was special about Rivera was not that he compiled more saves than any pitcher in history, not given the degraded nature of the stat, but for how long and how consistently he succeeded in the role. Among those who had seasons of 40 or more saves during his long tenure as Yankees closer included Eric Gagne, Jim Johnson, Jose Valverde, Brian Wilson, Jeff Shaw, Heath Bell, Mike Williams, and Joe Borowski. They came and went, but Rivera was still there long after they had risen and subsided. Thus he's fourth all-time in games pitched and first in games finished. And yet, we should also remember that he was never more valuable than he was in 1996, when Joe Torre used him for 107.2 innings of set-up relief, which is to say not to get saves.

MIKE MUSSINA, RHP (2001–2008)
Casey Stengel once said of the reliever Mike Marshall, "They say he's educated and he throws strikes. But what if you're educated and you don't throw strikes? Then they don't leave you in too long." Mussina was educated and he threw strikes. With a wide repertoire led by a knuckle curve and great command, "Moose" put together a long series of outstanding seasons that are only slightly obscured by the high-scoring era in which he pitched. His career ERA+ of 123 is not too different from Orioles' predecessor Jim Palmer's 125, but Palmer's actual ERA is more than three-quarters of a run lower due to his more beneficial environment. His Yankees years were a mix of excellence and struggles against onrushing age. He won that battle, winning 20 games, and then went home. The only thing that went missing was a Cy Young Award.

A Taxonomy of 2020 Abnormalities

by Rob Mains

I'm going to start this with a trivia question. Trust me, it's relevant. Don't bother skipping to the end of the article to find the answer, it's not there.

Only five players have appeared in 140 or more games for 16 straight seasons. Who are they?

It's a trivia question starting off an essay, so you know how this works: Whatever you guessed, you're wrong. It's okay. As someone who purchased this book, chances are good that you're an educated baseball fan. But the circumstances behind 2020 force us to abandon, or at least seriously question, some of our favorite patterns and crutches for evaluating the game we love.

We just completed what was undoubtedly the strangest season in MLB history. No fans, geographically limited schedule, universal DH, seven-inning twin bills, runners on second in extra innings, a 16-team postseason, a club playing at a Triple-A stadium. Some of these changes will likely persist (sorry), but we've never had so many tweaks dumped on us all at once, at least not since they figured out how many balls were in a walk.

And the biggest, of course, was the 60-game season. The 19th century was dotted with teams that went bankrupt before the season ended, but the lone season with only 60 scheduled games was 1877. That year there were only six teams, the league rostered a total of 77 players (just 16 more than the 2020 Marlins), and batters called for pitches to be thrown high or low by the pitcher, who was 50 feet away. We can say the 2020 season was easily the shortest ever for recognizable baseball.

As such, it'll stand out. Few abbreviated seasons do. Just about everybody reading this knows the 1994 season ended after Seattle's Randy Johnson struck out Oakland's Ernie Young for the last out of the Mariners-A's game on August 11. The ensuing player strike wiped out the rest of the season and the postseason. Teams played only 112-117 games that year.

And many of you know that a strike in the middle of the 1981 season split the season in two, resulting in the only Division Series until 1995. Teams played only 103-111 games that year, the shortest regular season since 1885.

Those two seasons are memorable. So when we see that nobody drove in 100 runs in 1981, or that Greg Maddux was the only pitcher with 180 or more innings pitched in 1994, we think, "Of course. Strike year."

But we don't remember other short years. You might not recall that the 1994 strike spilled into the next year, chopping 18 games off the 1995 schedule. You might've read that the 1918 season, played during the last pandemic, ended after Labor Day due to the government's World War I "work or fight" order. A strike erased the first week and a half of the 1972 season, but that year's best known as the last time pitchers batted in the American League.

The point is, while we don't remember small changes to the schedule, we remember the big ones. The 1981 mid-season strike. The 1994 season- and Series-ending strike. And, of course, the pandemic-shortened 2020 season. We won't need a reminder why Marcell Ozuna's 18 homers were the fewest to lead the National League in a century. (Literally; Cy Williams led with 15 in 1920.)

Now, about that trivia question. The five players are Hank Aaron, Brooks Robinson, Pete Rose, Ichiro Suzuki, and Johnny Damon. The one nobody gets, of course, is Damon, and a lot of people miss Ichiro, whose last season of 140-plus games came garbed in the red-orange and ocean blue of Miami when he was 42. That's half of what makes it a good question. The other half is the two guys whom many think made the list but didn't. Lou Gehrig? His streak started in the Yankees' 42nd game of the 1925 season and lasted only 13 seasons after that. And everybody assumes Cal Ripken Jr. did it, having played 2,632 straight games over 17 seasons. But one of those 17 seasons was 1994, when the Orioles played only 112 games.

My point? *I just told you* everybody remembers the 1994 strike year, but everybody forgets it fell in the middle of Ripken's streak, separating the first twelve years from the last four. Just because we recall something doesn't mean it's always at the front of our minds.

Nobody is going to forget 2020, and baseball is obviously not the main reason. But there will come a time in the future when you're looking at a player's or a team's record, and there will be baffling numbers there for 2020, and you'll think, "I wonder what happened." (Not to mention the missing line for minor league players.) Just like you forgot that the 1994 strike limited Ripken to 112 games.

Try not to forget it, though. The 2020 season resulted in weird statistical results for several reasons.

There were only 60 games.

I know, duh. But that had impacts beyond counting stats like Ozuna's home run total or Yu Darvish and Shane Bieber leading the majors with eight wins. (I know, pitcher wins, but still.)

The 162-game season is the longest among major North American sports, and that duration gives us a gift. Over the course of a long season, small variations tend to even out. A player who has a ten-game hot streak will probably have a ten-game cold streak. A team that starts the year losing a bunch of close games will probably win a bunch of them. We get regression to the mean. Statistics stabilize.

Consider flipping a coin. Over the long run, we expect it to come up heads about half the time. But the fewer flips, the more variation there'll be. If you flip a coin six times, probability theory tells us you'll get at least two-third heads about 34 percent of the time. Flip it 30 times, your chance of two-thirds heads drops to five percent.

Or, relevant to this case, if you flip a coin 60 times, your chance of getting at least 36 heads—that's 60 percent—is 7.75 percent. Expand the coin-flipping to 162 times, and the chance of getting 60 percent heads drops to 0.73 percent.

In other words, the odds of an outcome that's 20 percent better (or worse) than expected is *more than ten times higher* when you flip your coin 60 times than when you do it 162 times. Call it small sample size, call lack of mean reversion, or call it luck not evening out, 162 is a lot more predictive than 60. You get much more variation over 60 games than over 162. Bieber's 1.63 ERA and 0.87 FIP aren't something we'd see over a full season, and neither is Javier Baéz's .203/.238/.360.

Some players' lines in 2020 look normal. Brian Anderson had an .811 OPS in 2019 and an .810 OPS in 2020. (He probably would have gotten that last point if he'd been given enough time.) But there are many like Bieber and Baéz, some of them from young players still establishing their talent levels. The answer to the question, "What went right or wrong for that guy in 2020?" is most likely "Nothing, it was just a 2020 thing."

Preseason training was abbreviated for hitters.

Every year, spring training drags. Players get tired of it, fans get tired of it, and you sure can tell sportswriters get tired of it. Yes, something to get everyone into shape is necessary, but does it really have to drag on for over a month? Can't we shorten it?

The 2020 season answered in the negative, at least for hitters. Warren Spahn is credited with saying that hitting is timing and pitching is upsetting timing. It appears nobody had his timing down after the abbreviated July summer camp. Through August 9—18 games into the season—MLB batters were hitting .230/.311/.395 with a .275 BABIP. That BABIP, had it held, would have been the lowest since 1968, the Year of the Pitcher. In recent years it's hovered around .300.

It didn't hold. Play returned to more normal levels the rest of the year: .249/.325/.425 with a .297 BABIP starting August 10. But batters whose play concentrated in those first two weeks wound up with ugly lines. Andrew

Benintendi went on the injured list with a season-ending rib cage strain on August 11. His final line: .103/.314/.128 in 14 games. Franchy Cordero went on the IL with a hamate bone fracture on August 9 and a .154/.185/.231 line. Even though he came back strong in a late September return, it was too late to repair his full-season numbers.

Preseason training was abbreviated for pitchers.

Every year, spring training drags. Players get tired of it, fans get tired of it … wait, I already said that. But the abbreviated preseason was tough on pitchers, too. As noted, they had the upper hand coming out of the gate. But then they lost that hand. And then their arms, too.

The 2020 season was spread over 67 days. During those 67 days, 237 pitchers hit the Injured List, compared to 135 in the first 67 days of 2019. A lot of those IL stints, though, were COVID-19-related. Still, over the first 67 days of the 2019 season, there were 72 pitchers on the IL with arm injuries. That figure jumped to 110 in 2020, a 53 percent increase.

There are a number of factors contributing to pitcher arm injuries, ranging from usage to velocity, but it appears that attenuated preseason training played a role. A lot of pitchers had super-short seasons due to arm woes. Corey Kluber, Roberto Osuna, and Shohei Ohtani combined for seven innings, none after August 8. All suffered arm injuries. We'll never know whether they'd have fared better with a longer preseason, but we can guess how they probably feel.

Everybody played.

Rosters were set to expand from 25 to 26 in 2020, so even if we'd had a normal season, we'd have likely seen 2019's record of 1,410 players on MLB rosters broken. But due to the pandemic, rosters started the year at 30 and were cut to only 28. Add multiple COVID-19 absences and the revolving door caused by poor starts by hitters and a rash of pitcher arm injuries, and 1,289 players appeared in MLB games in 2020. The comparable figure over the first 67 days of the 2019 season was 1,109. That 16 percent increase works out to an average of six more players per team in 2020 compared to a similar slice of 2019. A future look back at 2020 rosters will include a lot of unfamiliar names.

Plus became a minus.

In advanced metrics, we adjust batter and pitcher performance for park and league/era variations. A plus sign appended to the end of a measure means that it's adjusted for park and league. It's scaled to an average of 100, with higher figures above average and lower figures below average. (Similarly, a metric with a minus is also park- and league-adjusted and scaled to 100, with lower values better.) Here at BP, our advanced measure of offensive performance is DRC+. Baseball-Reference has OPS+ and FanGraphs has wRC+.

Using park and league adjustments, we can compare Dante Bichette's 1995 Steroid Era season at pre-humidor Coors Field (.340/.364/.620, 40 homers, 128 RBI, MVP runner-up) with Jim Wynn's 1968 Year of the Pitcher season at the cavernous Astrodome (.269/.376/.474, 26 homers, 67 RBI, no MVP votes). It's not close. DRC+, OPS+, and wRC+ all give the nod to Wynn, handily. This is a useful tool. As my Baseball Prospectus colleague Patrick Dubuque tweeted last fall, "Please note that when I ask how you are, I am already adjusting for era."

The 2020 season messes up plus (and minus) stats for two reasons. First, the park adjustment was based on only 30 home games instead of the usual 81. Everything noted above regarding the short season applies, literally doubly, to park effect calculations. DRC+ uses a single-season park factor. OPS+ uses a three-year average and wRC+ five years. The figure for 2020 is suspect.

Second, OPS+ and wRC+ adjust for league: American and National. (DRC+ adjusts for opponent, regardless of league.) While there were two leagues in 2020, they were an artificial construct. To reduce travel, teams played opponents geographically, not based on league. There weren't two leagues, American and National. There were three, Western, Central, and Eastern.

That makes a difference because teams in the same league played in different run-scoring environments. AL teams scored 4.58 runs per game, NL teams 4.71. That's a small difference. But teams in the East scored 0.21 more runs per game (4.95) than teams in the West (4.74), and they both scored a lot more than Central teams (4.25). Adjusting for league misses that difference, so this book will be safe in that regard, but other sources may be distorted somewhat.

Not every game was a "game."

In 2020, the rising tide of strikeouts was finally stemmed. Strikeouts per team per game fell from 8.8 in 2019 to 8.7 in 2020. That marked the first decline after 14 straight annual increases.

In 2020, the rising tide of strikeouts rose higher. Batters struck out in 23.4 percent of plate appearances compared to 23.0 percent in 2019. That marked the 15th straight annual increase.

Both are true statements.

Because of two rule changes—seven-inning doubleheaders and runners on second in extra innings—games in 2020 were unprecedented in their brevity. There were 37.0 plate appearances per game in 2020. The only years with fewer were 1904 and 1906-1909. The average game in 2020 entailed 8.61 innings pitched, the fewest since 1899.

So when you see any per-game stats for 2020, you need to increase them by 3 or 4 percent to get them on equal footing with recent years.

Or, better, just ignore them. Last year happened. There were major league games contested between major league teams. But when you're looking at those physical or electronic baseball cards, when you're weaving narratives over why this young player's inevitable rise to stardom fell apart or why that old veteran rekindled his magic, don't linger on the 2020 line. It was just too weird.

Thanks to Lucas Apostoleris for research assistance.

—*Rob Mains is an author of Baseball Prospectus.*

Tranches of WAR

by Russell A. Carleton

We ask "replacement level" to be a lot of things. Sometimes contradictory things. Sometimes I wonder if we know what it even means anymore. The original idea was that it represented the level of production that a team could expect to get from "freely available talent", including bench players, minor leaguers, and waiver wire pickups. It created a common benchmark to compare everyone to, and for that reason, it represented an advancement well beyond what was available at the time. In fact, it created a language and a framework for evaluating players that was not just better but *entirely* different than what came before it.

But then we started mumbling in that language. The idea behind "wins above replacement" was one part sci-fi episode and one part mathematical exercise. Imagine that a player had disappeared before the season and suddenly, in an alternate timeline, his team would have had to replace him. The distance between him and that replacement line was his value. We need to talk about that alternate timeline.

Without getting too into 2:00 am "deep conversations" with extensive navel-gazing, it's worth thinking about why one player might not be playing, while another might.

- A player might not be playing because he has a short-term injury or his manager believes that he needs a day off.
- A player might not be playing because he has a longer-term injury that requires him to be on the injured list.

There's a difference here between these two situations. In particular, the first one generally *doesn't* involve a compensatory roster move, while the second one does. It's possible, though not guaranteed, that the person who will be replacing the injured/resting player would be the same in either case. That matters. Teams generally carry a spare part for all eight position players on the diamond, although in the era of a four-player bench, those spare parts usually are the backup plan for more than one spot.

New York Yankees 2021

A couple of years ago, I posed a hypothetical question. Suppose that a team had two players in its system fighting for a fourth outfielder spot. One of them was a league average hitter, but would be worth 20 runs below average if allowed to play center field for a full season. One of them was a perfectly average fielder, but would be 15 runs below average as a hitter, if allowed to play an entire season. Which of the two should the team roster? It's tempting to say the second one, as overall, he is the better player. That misses the point. A league average hitter on the bench isn't just a potential replacement for an injured outfielder. He might also pinch hit for the light-hitting shortstop in a key spot. You keep the average hitter on the roster, even though he isn't a hand-in-glove fit for one specific place on the field, because being a bench player is a different job description than being a long-term fill-in for someone. If you find yourself in need of a longer-term fill-in, you can bring the other guy up from AAA.

When we're determining the value of an everyday player though, if he had disappeared before the season and a team would have had to replace his production, they likely would have done it with a player who was a long-term fill-in type because they would have had to replace a guy who played everyday. Maybe that's the same guy that they would have rostered on their bench anyway, but we don't know. It gets to the query of what we hope to accomplish with WAR. Are we looking for an accurate modeling of reality or are we looking for a common baseline to compare everyone to? Both have their uses, but they are somewhat different questions.

Let's talk about another dichotomy.

- A player might not be playing because he isn't very good and is a bench-level player.
- A player might not be playing because there is another player on the team who has a situational advantage that makes him the better choice today. The classic case of this is a handedness platoon. On another day, he might be a better choice.

When we think about player usage, I think we're still stuck in the model that there are starters and there are scrubs. We have plenty of words for bench players or reserves or backups or utility guys. We do still have the word "platoon" in our collective vocabulary, but in the age of short benches, it's hard to construct one. It's always been hard to construct them. You have to find two players who hit with different hands, have skill sets that complement each other, and probably play the same position. In the era of the short bench, one of them had probably better double as a utility player in some way. Baseball has a two-tiered language geared toward the idea of regulars and reserves. The fact that it was so easy for me to find plenty of synonyms for "a player whose primary function is to come into a game to replace a regular player if he is injured or resting" should tell you something.

I'm always one to look for "unspoken words" in baseball. What is it called when someone is both half of a platoon and the utility infielder? That guy exists sometimes, but he reveals himself in that role—usually by accident. We don't have a word for that, and whenever I find myself saying "we don't have a word for that", I look for new opportunities. What do you call it, further, when the job of being the utility infielder is decentralized across the whole infield with occasional contributions from the left fielder? It's not even a "super-utility" player. What happens when you build your entire roster around the idea that everyone will be expected to be a triple major?

⚾ ⚾ ⚾

I think someone else beat me to this one, and on a grand scale. Platoons work because we know that hitters of the opposite hand to the pitcher get better results than hitters of the same hand, usually to the tune of about 20 points of OBP. If you want to express that in runs, it usually comes out to somewhere around 10 to 12 runs of linear weights value prorated across 650 PA. But hang on a second, now let's say that we have two players who might start today, both of roughly equal merit with the bat. One has a handedness advantage, but is the worse fielder of the two. In that case, as long as his "over the course of a season" projection as a fielder at whatever position you want to slot him into is less than a 10-run drop from the guy he might replace, then he's a better option today.

We're not used to thinking of utility players as bat-first options, who would play below-average defense at three different infield positions. That guy might hook on as a 2B/3B/LF type (Howie Kendrick, come on down!) but teams usually think to themselves that they need as their utility infielder someone who "can handle" shortstop, the toughest of the infield spots to play. If someone can do that *and* hit well, he's probably already starting somewhere, so he's not available as a utility infielder. It's easier for those glove guys to find a job. In a world where the replacement for a shortstop *has to be* the designated utility infielder, that makes sense.

But as we talked about last week, we're living in a different world. The rate at which a replacement for a regular starter turns out to be *another starter* shifting over to cover has gone way up over the last five years. There was always some of it in the game, but this has been a supernova of switcheroos. Now if your second baseman is capable of playing a decent shortstop, that 2B/3B/LF guy can swap in. He's not actually playing shortstop, and maybe the defense suffers from the switch, but if he's got enough of a bat, he might outhit those extra fielding miscues. And in doing so, he is effectively your backup shortstop.

Somewhere along the lines, teams got hip to the idea of multi-positional play from their regulars. I've written before about how you can't just put a player, however athletic, into a new position and expect much at first. The data tell us that. Eventually, players can learn to be multi-positionalists, but it takes time, roughly on the order of two months, before they're OK. But there's a hidden message in there. If you give a player some reps at a new spot, he's a reasonably gifted athlete and somewhat smart and willing to learn, he could probably pick it up enough to get to "good enough," and it doesn't take forever. You just have to be purposeful about it. Maybe you get to the point where you can start to say "he's still below average but we could move him there and get another bat into the lineup, and it's a net win."

Teams have started to build those extra lessons into their player development program. It used to be seen as a mark of weakness to be relegated to "utility player" because that meant that you were a bench player (all those synonyms above come with a side of stigma). Now, it's a way of building a team. If you get a few reps in the minors (where it doesn't count) at a spot, you'll have at least played the spot at game speed before. There are limits to how far you can push that. A slow-footed "he's out in left field because we don't have the DH" guy is never going to play short, but maybe your third baseman can try second base and not look like a total moose out there.

⚾ ⚾ ⚾

Back to WAR. I'd argue that the world of starters and scrubs is slowly disintegrating, for good cause. In the event that a regular starter really does go down with an injury–ostensibly, the alternate universe scenario that WAR is attempting to model–it makes the team a little more resilient to replacing him. And the good news is that you're more likely to be able to replace him with the best of the bench bunch, rather than the third-best guy, because the best guy doesn't have to be an exact positional match for the guy who got hurt. And that's what the manager would want to do. He'd want to replace that long-term production, not with an amalgam of everyone else who played that position, but with the best guy available from his reserves.

Now this is still WAR. We still want to retain the principle that we should be measuring a player, and not his teammates. We need some sort of common baseline, and despite what I just said, we'll still need some sort of amalgam. To construct that, I give to you the idea of the tranche. The word, if you've not heard it before, refers to a piece of a whole that is somehow segmented off. It's often used in finance to talk about layers of a financial instrument.

Here, I want you to consider that there are 30 starters at each of the seven non-battery positions (catchers should have their own WAR, since only a catcher can replace a catcher). We can identify them by playing time, and we can futz around with the definition a little bit if we need to. Next, among those who aren't in that starting pool, we identify the top tranche of the 30 best bench players, which I would again identify by playing time, and then the second and third and fourth and so on. If a player were to disappear, his manager would probably want to take a guy from that top tranche of the bench to replace him. In a world where even the starters can slide around the field, that becomes more feasible.

We can take a look at that top tranche and say "How many of them showed that they are able to play (first, second, etc.)?" and therefore could have directly substituted for the starter? How many of them could have been a direct substitute for our injured player? We don't know whether one of them would be on *a specific* team, but we can say that 40 percent of the time, a manager would have been able to draw from tranche 1 in filling the role, and 35 percent from tranche 2. But on tranche 1, we can also look at how many of those players played a position that could have then shifted and covered for that spot. We'd need some eligibility criteria for all of this (probably a minimum number of games played) but it would just be a matter of multiplication. Shortstop would be harder to fill, and managers would probably be dipping a little further down in the talent pool, and so replacement level would be lower, as it is now.

Doing some quick analysis, I found that the difference in just batting linear weights (haven't even gotten into running or fielding) between tranche 1 and tranche 2 in 2019 was about 6.5 runs, prorated across 650 PA. Between tranche 1 and tranche 3, it's 10.8 runs. The ability to shift those plate appearances up the ladder has some real value.

This part is important. We can also give credit to starters for the positions that they showed an ability to play, even if they didn't play them (this is the guy fully capable of playing center, but who's in a corner because the team already has a good center fielder) because he allows a team to carry a player who hits like a left fielder to functionally be the team's backup center fielder. He facilitates that movement upward among the tranches. We can start to appreciate the difference between a left fielder who would never be able to hack it in center (and the compensatory move that his team would have to make) and the left fielder who could do it, but just didn't have to very often.

Past that, you can continue to use whatever hitting and fielding and running metrics you like to determine a player's value, but when we get down to constructing that baseline, I'd argue we need a better conceptual and mathematical framework. It's going to require some more #GoryMath than we're used to, but I'd argue it's a better conceptualization of the way that MLB actually plays the game in 2020. If…y'know…MLB plays in 2020. If WAR is going to be our flagship statistic among the *acronymati*, then we need to acknowledge that it contains some old and starting-to-be-out-of-date assumptions about the game. We may need to tinker with it. Here's my idea for how.

—*Russell A. Carleton is an author of Baseball Prospectus.*

Secondhand Sport

by Patrick Dubuque

Back before time stopped, I liked to go to thrift stores. Now that I'm older, I rarely ever buy anything—I don't need much in my life, now—but I still enjoy the old familiar circuit: check to see if there are baseball cards to write about, look for board or card games to play with the kids, scan for random ironic jerseys, hit the book section. It takes ten, maybe fifteen minutes. Thrift stores are the antithesis of modern online shopping, because you don't know what they have, and you don't even really know what you want. It's junk, literal junk, stuff other people thought was worthless. That's what makes it great.

In an idealized economy, thrift stores shouldn't exist. Everybody has a living wage, and every product has a durability that exactly matches its desired life; nothing should need to be given away, no one should need to be given to. But then, thrift stores shouldn't work on a customer experience level, either. You wouldn't think an ethos of "let's make everything disorganized and hard to find" would lead to customer satisfaction, but low-budget retailers like TJ Maxx and Ross thrive on this model. People like bargain hunting as much for the hunting as the bargain; it's part of the experience, spending time as if it's a wager. There's a thrill, occasionally, in inefficiency.

In sports, the modern overuse of the word "inefficiency" is a condemnation: It insinuates that there is *an* efficiency, a correct way to be found, and that all other ways are wrong ways. It's prevalent in baseball but hardly contained to it; the lifehack, the Silicon Valley disruption are other examples of productivity creep in our daily lives. Their modern success makes plenty of sense. Maximization of resources, after all, is its own puzzle, and an industry of European board games is founded upon it. It's fun to take a system and optimize it, unravel it like a sudoku puzzle. If there's only one kind of genius, after all, there's no way anyone can fail to appreciate it.

Baseball has been hacking away at these perceived inefficiencies since its inception: platoons, bullpens, farm systems were all installed to extract more out of the tools at hand. But it's been a particular badge of the sabermetric movement, from Ken Phelps and his All-Star Team to Ricardo Rincon and the darlings of *Moneyball*. It's business, but it's also an ethos: the idea that there's treasure among the trash, something we all failed to appreciate until someone brought it to light.

It's the myth that made Sidd Finch so enticing, that fuels so many "best shape" narratives and new pitch promises. We all, athletes and unathletic sportswriters, want to believe that there's genius trapped inside us, and that it's just a matter of puzzling out the combination to unlock it. That our art, our style is the next inefficiency, waiting for our own Billy Beane. It's why we root for underdogs, and why we're excited for the Mike Tauchmans and the Eurubiel Durazos, champions of skin-deep mediocrity.

Except we aren't anymore, really. The days of "Free X" have descended beyond the ring of irony and into obscurity. There are still Xs to be freed, or at least one X, duplicated endlessly: Mike Ford, Luke Voit, Max Muncy. The undervalued one-dimensional slugger demonstrated how the game hasn't quite culturally caught up to its logical extreme. But for those who don't fit the rather spacious mold, times are grimmer. As Rob Arthur revealed several months ago, there's been a marked increase in the number of sub-replacement relievers. It's the outcome of a greater number of teams forced to play out games without the talent to win them, but it's also emblematic of the modern tendency of teams to dispose of their disposable assets, burning through cost-controlled arms the way that man chopped down forests in *The Lorax*. Stuff just isn't built to outlive their original owners anymore.

It's unsurprising, given how well-mined the market for inefficiencies has been of late. The disciples of the early analytics departments, and the disciples of those, have proliferated the league, with only a few backwater holdouts. The league has grown smarter, but every team has learned the same lesson. In fact, the phenomenon creates a peculiar kind of feedback loop: As teams value a specific subset of players or skills, prospective athletes learn to increase their own marketability by conforming themselves to the demands of their prospective employers.

And that's tragic, in the way that the extinction of animals is tragic; a certain amount of biodiversity in baseball has been lost. Shortstops hit like outfielders. Pitchers don't hit at all. Only the catchers remain idiosyncratic, thanks to the defensive demands of their position; eventually they too will be required to produce like everyone else, or they'll meet the fate of their battery mates. A perfect economy requires perfect production.

I mentioned earlier that more and more, I leave thrift stores empty-handed. It is true that I am more discerning than in the past; my bookshelves are full, and there are more streaming films than I will ever be able to watch. But there are other factors at play.

Thrift stores are, in a way, the bond markets of retail. When the economy is rough and other retailers are struggling, more people look secondhand for their products. But as recently as last year, publications were noting a reversal of the trend: Companies like Goodwill and Savers were expanding despite a strong economy. Publications credited a heightened sense of environmentalism and a rejection of cutting-edge fashion as drivers behind the increase, though the more likely answer is the modern American economy hasn't showered its favors equally, particularly among the young.

But it is more than just the economy. Baseball and thrift stores share something else in common, evident in our current conversations about re-starting the sport: They live in the gray area between public service and private enterprise. Thrift stores provide affordable necessities to lower-class citizens, and collectibles and fashion for the middle-class. Because of the success of the latter, prices have gone up across the board. Especially in terms of clothing, the middle-class flight from fashion into vintage has instead carried the aftereffects of fashion, including its costs, into a territory where people just want clothes. But there's another factor in the rise of prices, in the form of the internet.

The Goodwills of the world have grown smarter, too, employing the internet to extract full value from their detritus. Ebay, similarly, has lost much of the charm it had as a new frontier around the turn of the century. Everything has a price point now; even individual taste is no match for the algorithm, because anything rare, no matter how niche its market, is a collectible to someone.

The internet has had the same effect on thrift stores that sabermetrics has had on baseball; its equivalent to OBP was the bar scanner. As detailed in Slate, the rise of second-party stores on eBay and Amazon birthed an entire industry of used-good salespeople, armed with PDAs and scanners, buying books for three dollars to sell online for five. The author, Michael Savitz, reports earning $60,000 by working nearly 80 hours a week; he makes it clear that this is not a vocation of his choosing. It's long hours, with no real creativity or individuality, skimming the cream off of a local establishment and flipping it to someone with a little more money on the other side of the country. And once the vocation exists, the obvious question arises: why wait to put the wares out on the shelves? Why allow value to exist at all?

Nothing is ruined. Thrift stores will continue to sell polo shirts and DVDs, and baseball will continue to exist and make or lose money, depending on who you believe. But as we continue to refine our knowledge, we lose something in the conquest for efficiency, a delight born out of the unknown. The problem isn't the efficiency itself; we can't blame the booksellers, or the people sweeping freeways to collect grams of platinum from damaged catalytic converters. The problem is a system that requires this sort of profit-skimming behavior in order to feed families (or, for corporations, maximize shareholder return).

In times like these, with the 2020 season on the brink and the collective bargaining agreement close behind, it can often feel like the current situation is untenable. It can't keep going like this, even if we don't know what to do about it. But as with thrift stores, there's an equally irresistible feeling that it *has* to keep going, that it would be unimaginable to not have this broken, amazing sport. Both industries exist on an invisible foundation of friction, of chaos and unpredictability, even as both see their foundations buffed down to a perfect, untouchable polish. But if COVID-19 and its financial ramifications do, as some have suggested, make it such that the baseball that returns is fundamentally different than the baseball that came before, perhaps this is the time to lean in, and change the game even more. Fix bunting. Make defense more difficult. Create viable, alternate strategies. Add some chaos back into baseball. It's fun when no one knows quite where things are.

—Patrick Dubuque is an author of Baseball Prospectus.

Steve Dalkowski Dreaming

by Steven Goldman

We dream of being a pitcher, of starring in the major leagues. Depending on your age and your sense of historical perspective, you might imagine yourself as Walter Johnson, throwing harder than anyone else—hitting more batters than anyone else, too, but always feeling bad about it. You could picture yourself as a Tom Seaver or a David Cone, with all the stuff in the world but still being cerebral about it, thinking about so much more than burning 'em in there. There are so many models one could choose: You could be a Lefty Gomez, Jim Bouton, or Bill Lee, skilled, but not taking the whole thing too seriously, or a Lefty Grove, Bob Gibson, or Steve Carlton, powerful but treating each start like a mission to be survived instead of a game to be enjoyed.

Very few would dream of being Steve Dalkowski, the former Baltimore Orioles prospect who died of COVID-19 last week at the age of 80. Yet, there is something just as noble in Dalkowski's negative accomplishments—and accomplishments is what they are—as there is in the precision-engineered pitching of a Greg Maddux. You have to be very good to be that bad. Dalkowski had all of the stuff of the greatest pitchers but none of the command; his story is not one of failing to conquer his limitations, but striving against one of the cruelest hands that fate or genetics or personality can deal us: A desire to achieve great things which is almost but not quite matched by the ability to meet that goal.

As with Johnson, Grove, Bob Feller, and the rest of the hard-throwing pitchers who played before the advent of modern radar guns, we have to take the word of the players and coaches who saw Dalkowski pitch as to his velocity. He was a hard-drinking, maximum-effort pitcher who, if their memories are to be believed, consistently threw over 100 miles per hour. His was the Maltese Fastball, the stuff that dreams are made of. The problem is that velocity without command and control is still a good distance from utility. Dalkowski was the most effective towel you could design for a fish, the sleekest bathing suit intended to be worn by an astronaut, but that doesn't mean he wasn't beautiful: We can appreciate a journey even if it doesn't end at the intended destination.

Whether because of sloppy mechanics he couldn't calm, an inability to understand that a consistent 98 in the strike zone would likely be more effective than a consistent 110 out of it, or all that beer, Dalkowski could never make the adjustments that pitchers like Feller and Nolan Ryan made before him, possibly because he had so far to go: Feller, who never pitched in the minors, came up at 17 and spent three years walking almost seven batters per nine innings before settling in at 3.8 beginning when he was 20. Ryan started out walking over six batters per nine but gradually improved as his long career played out; for him to go from 6.2 walks per nine with the 1966 Greenville Mets to 3.7 with the 1989 Texas Rangers represents a 40 percent reduction. An equivalent improvement by Dalkowski would still have left him walking over 11 batters per nine innings.

Dalkowski was like *The Room* of pitchers, a player so bad he became good again. Cal Ripken, Sr., who both played with and managed Dalkowski, recalled in a 1979 *Sporting News* "where are they now" piece the occasion when the pitcher crossed up his catcher and his fastball, "hit the plate umpire smack in the mask. The mask broke all to pieces and the umpire wound up in the hospital for three days with a concussion. If they ever had a radar gun in those days, I'll bet Dalkowski would have been timed at 110 miles an hour."

Signed by the Orioles out of New Britain High in Connecticut in 1957, Dalkowski was sent to Kingsport in the Appalachian League, where he pitched 62 innings. He allowed only 22 hits in 62 innings, or 3.2 per nine, a number with no equivalent in major league history (though Aroldis Chapman came close in 2014), and also struck out 121 (17.6 per nine) and walked 129 (18.7). He was also charged with 39 wild pitches. That June, one of his fastballs clipped a Dodgers prospect named Bob Beavers and carried away part of his ear. "The first pitch was over the backstop, the second pitch was called a strike, I didn't think it was," Beavers said last year. "The third pitch hit me and knocked me out, so I don't remember much after that. I couldn't get in the sun for a while, and I never did play baseball again." Former minor leaguer Ron Shelton based the *Bull Durham* pitcher Nuke LaLoosh on Dalkowski. And yet, to see him as a figure of fun, an amusing loser, is to misunderstand something unique and strange.

Dalkowski kept on posting some of the strangest lines in baseball history. Pitching for the Stockton Ports of the Class C California League in 1960, he struck out 262 and walked 262 in 170 innings. Yet, he did improve, especially after pitching for Earl Weaver at Elmira in 1962. Weaver had previously had Dalkowski at Aberdeen in 1959, but wasn't ready to grapple with him then. This time he was. "I had grown more and more concerned about players with great physical abilities who could not learn to correct certain basic deficiencies no matter how much you instructed or drilled them," he related in his autobiography, *It's What You Learn After You Know It All That Counts*. He got permission from the Orioles to give all of his players the Stanford-Binet IQ test. "Dalkowski finished in the 1 percentile in his ability to understand facts. Steve, it was said to say, had the ability to do everything but learn." [sic]

IQ tests are problematic diagnostic tools, so take Weaver's estimate of Dalkowski's mental capabilities with a grain of salt. What's important is that even if he got to the right answer by way of the wrong reason, Weaver had learned something valuable. His insight was to stop asking Dalkowski to learn new pitches and just let him get by with the two that he had. Were Dalkowski a prospect today, that would have been a no-brainer: Can't develop a third pitch? The bullpen is right over there, sir. Player development wasn't like that then, but Weaver, temporarily Dalkowski's mentor, could let him work with what he had. According to Weaver, the pitcher responded: "In the final 57 innings he pitched that season Dalkowski gave up 1 earned run, struck out 110 batters, and walked only 11." It's not true—as per the *Elmira Star-Gazette*, as of late July, Dalkowski had walked 71 in 106 innings and finished with 114 in 160 innings, which means Dalkowski's control actually faded at the end of the season rather than improved—but that doesn't mean it didn't happen in some sense, just that it didn't happen that way. Again, it's the journey, not the destination, and his ERA was 3.04 so *something* had gone right.

Also along the way: The next spring, Orioles manager Billy Hitchcock was rooting for Dalkowski to make the team as a long-man—maybe Weaver had gotten through to him. There were things out of Weaver's control, like the universe's twisted sense of humor: that March, Dalkowski's elbow went "twang."

You sometimes read that it was the Orioles' insistence on Dalkowski learning the curve that did him in, but even if they hadn't learned their lesson, the injury was probably just a coincidence: Dalkowski had thrown an incredible number of pitches over the previous few years. Still, it testifies to the dangers of trying to get what you want and risking the loss of what you had. Dalkowski tried to come back, but the 110-mph stuff was gone. A pitcher with no control and no stuff is…a civilian. What followed were years of vagabond living, arrests for drunkenness. There were Alcoholics Anonymous meetings, assistance from baseball alumni associations, but none of it took. From the 1990s until the time of his passing he dwelt in an assisted living facility, suffering from alcohol-related dementia. He'd been a heavy drinker since his teenage years. As with all those pitches per game, there was a price to be paid. You make choices on the journey and some of them are irrevocable. It's like a fairy tale: "Bite of poison apple? Don't mind if I do."

In the aforementioned *Sporting News* profile, Chuck Stevens, the head of the Association of Professional Ballplayers of America, a ballplayer charity, said, "I've got nothing against drinking. I do it myself sometimes. But, I don't condone common drunkenness. We went through lots of heartache and many dollars, but Dalkowski didn't want to help himself and we weren't going to keep him drunk." The journey is *un*like a fairy tale: No one will come along and kiss it better, not if they're busy forming judgments.

In the end, we are left with a sort of philosophical chicken/egg conundrum: Is failing to meet your goals evidence of unfulfilled potential or the lack of it? Isn't what you did by definition what you were capable of doing? Or could you have broken through to something better with the right help, the right lucky break? These are unanswerable questions, and how we try to answer them may say more about us than about the people we're judging.

No pitcher ever has it easy. *All* pitchers must work hard. *All* pitchers must refine their craft. It's almost never just about *stuff*. Dalkowski dreaming is no insult to the great pitchers who made it; from Pete Alexander to Max Scherzer, they have all earned their way up. And yet, if it is true that we can only do as much as we can do, then the journey would be more of an adventure, the ultimate triumph or defeat more noble, if like Dalkowski we lacked 100 percent of the confidence, the command, the self-possession, the commitment, the resistance to making bad decisions that so many great players possess—to be gloriously human. Or, to put it more succinctly, it would be fun to be able to throw as hard as any person ever has. Even if just for a moment, and even if nothing more came of it than that, no one could say you hadn't lived life to the fullest.

—Steven Goldman is an author of Baseball Prospectus.

A Reward For A Functioning Society

by Cory Frontin and Craig Goldstein

On July 5, Nationals reliever Sean Doolittle said in the middle of a press conference regarding the restart of Major League Baseball and what would later be known as summer camp, "sports are like the reward of a functioning society." This sentence was amidst a much longer, thoughtful reply about the societal and health conditions under which MLB players were being brought back. It's a very similar sentiment to one Jane McManus used on April 7, when she discussed the White House's meeting with sports commissioners. She said "sports are the effect of a functioning society—not the precursor."

Both versions of the same sentiment spoke to a laudable ideal in the context of a country that was not addressing a rampaging virus, and opting instead to bring sports back for the feeling of normalcy rather than the reality of it. "Priorities," as McManus said.

On Wednesday, the NBA's Milwaukee Bucks conducted a wildcat/political strike, refusing to come out for Game 5 of their playoff series against the Orlando Magic. The Magic refused to accept the forfeit, and shortly thereafter other playoff series were threatened by player strikes. Eventually the league moved to postpone that day's games, folding to players leveraging their united power.

The backdrop against which these actions took place was the shooting by police of Jacob Blake. Blake was shot in the back seven times by police, as he attempted to get into his vehicle. He managed to survive the assault, but is paralyzed from the waist down.

⚾ ⚾ ⚾

The step taken to walk out, first by the Milwaukee Bucks, then subsequently by other NBA, WNBA, and MLB teams, was a step toward upholding the virtue of the sentiment described by McManus and Doolittle. But that sentiment does not align with the broad history of sports in this and other countries, a history that contradicts the core of the idealistic statement.

Sports have been a significant part of American society for most of its existence, expanding in importance and influence in recent years. The idea that society was functioning in a way that was worthy of the reward of sports for most of that time is laughable. Much of America is not functioning and has not functioned for Black people, full stop. The oppressed people at the center of this political act by players, specifically Black players, in concert throughout the NBA and in fits and starts throughout Major League Baseball, have not known a society that functions for them rather than *because* of them.

Politics has been part of the sports landscape since the inception of sport, but for just about as long people have bemoaned its presence. Sports are to be an escape, it is said. An escape from what, though? A functioning society?

No, the presence of sports has never signified a cultural or political system that is on the up and up. Rather, the presence of sports *reflect and reinforce the society* that produces them.

⚾   ⚾   ⚾

The Negro Leagues were born out of societal dysfunction. The need for entirely separate leagues, composed of Black and Latino players barred from the Major Leagues because of racism? That is not a functioning society, and yet there were sports.

Even the integration of players from the Negro Leagues resulted in a transfer of power and wealth from Black-owned businesses and communities and into white ones, mirroring the dysfunction that had bled into every aspect of American society at the time. Japheth Knopp noted in the Spring 2016 Baseball Research Journal:

> *The manner in which integration in baseball—and in American businesses generally—occurred was not the only model which was possible. It was likely not even the best approach available, but rather served the needs of those in already privileged positions who were able to control not only the manner in which desegregation occurred, but the public perception of it as well in order to exploit the situation for financial gain. Indeed, the very word integration may not be the most applicable in this context because what actually transpired was not so much the fair and equitable combination of two subcultures into one equal and more homogenous group, but rather the reluctant allowance—under certain preconditions—for African Americans to be assimilated into white society.*

To understand the value of a movement, though, is not to understand how it is co-opted by ownership, but to know the people it brings together and what they demand. When Jackie Robinson—the player who demarcated the inevitability of the end of the Negro leagues—attended the March on Washington for Jobs and Freedom in 1963, he did so with his family and marched alongside the people. He stood alongside hundreds of thousands to fight for their common civil and labor rights. "The moral arc of the universe is long," many freedom fighters have echoed, "but it bends towards justice." The bend, it is less frequently said, happens when a great mass of people place the moral arc of the universe on their knee and apply force, as Jackie, his family, and thousands of others did that day.

⚾ ⚾ ⚾

Of course, taking the moral arc of the universe down from the mantle and bending it is not without risk. Perhaps the outsized influence of athletes is itself a mark of a dysfunctional society, but, nonetheless, hundreds of athletes woke up on Wednesday morning with the power to bring in millions of dollars in revenues. That very power, as we would come to find out, was matched with the equal and opposite power to *not* bring those revenues. That power, in hands ranging from the Milwaukee Bucks, to Kenny Smith in the *Inside the NBA* Studio, from the unexpected ally, Josh Hader, and his largely white teammates to the notably Black Seattle Mariners, would be exercised for a single demand: the end to state violence against Black people. Not unlike the March itself, it sat at the intersection of the civil rights of Black Americans and bold labor action. The March on Washington stood in the face of a false notion of integration—against an integration of extraction but not one of equality—and proposed something different. Just the same, the acts of solidarity of August 26, 2020 will be remembered in stark defiance of MLB's BLM-branded, but ultimately empty displays on opening weekend.

Bold defiance like this can never be without risk. By choosing to exercise this power, the Milwaukee Bucks took a risk. They risked vitriol and backlash from those they disagreed with. They risked fines or seeing their contracts voided, as a walkout like this is prohibited by their CBA. They risked forfeiting a playoff game, one that, as the No. 1 seed in the playoffs, they'd worked all year to attain. They didn't know how Orlando would respond. It wasn't clear that other teams throughout the league would follow suit in solidarity. And it wasn't known the league would accept these actions and moderately co-opt them by "postponing" games that would have featured no players.

If the league reschedules the games, some of the athletes' risk—their shared sacrifice—will be diminished, in retrospect. But they did not know any of that when they took that risk. And it is often left to athletes to take these risks when others in society won't, especially those of their same socioeconomic status and levels of influence.

It is athletes, specifically BIPOC athletes, that take them, though, because they live with the risk of being something other than white in this country every day. They are no strangers to the realities of police brutality. It seems incongruous

New York Yankees 2021

then, to say that sports are a reward for a functioning society when we rely on athletes to lead us closer to being a functioning society. Luckily, our beloved athletes, WNBA players first and foremost among them, understand what sports truly are: a pipebender for the moral arc of the universe.

> —*Craig Goldstein is editor in chief of Baseball Prospectus. Cory Frontin is an author of Baseball Prospectus.*

Index of Names

Abreu, Albert 78, 98
Alcantara, Kevin 68, 94
Allen, Greg 68
Andújar, Miguel 16
Bowman, Matt 78
Breaux, Josh 96
Brito, Socrates 69
Britton, Zack 42
Cessa, Luis 44
Chacín, Jhoulys 79
Chapman, Aroldis 46
Cole, Gerrit 48
Contreras, Roansy 96
Cortes, Nestor 80
Dominguez, Jasson 70, 90
Duran, Ezequiel 70, 95
Escotto, Maikol 97
Estrada, Thairo 71
Florial, Estevan 72, 92
Ford, Mike 72
Frazier, Clint 18
Garcia, Deivi 50, 89
Gardner, Brett 20
Germán, Domingo 81
Gil, Luis 82, 91
Green, Chad 52
Heller, Ben 82
Herrera, Rosell 73
Hicks, Aaron 22
Higashioka, Kyle 24
Judge, Aaron 26
King, Michael 54
Kluber, Corey 83
Kratz, Erik 28
Kriske, Brooks 56
LeMahieu, DJ 30
Loaisiga, Jonathan 58
Medina, Luis 84, 92
Montgomery, Jordan 60
Nelson, Nick 62
O'Day, Darren 64
Paxton, James 85
Peraza, Oswald 97
Sánchez, Gary 74
Schmidt, Clarke 86, 90
Seigler, Anthony 98
Severino, Luis 87
Sikkema, T.J. 98
Stanton, Giancarlo 32
Taillon, Jameson 88
Tanaka, Masahiro 66
Tauchman, Mike 75
Torres, Gleyber 34
Urshela, Gio 36
Vargas, Alexander 97
Velazquez, Andrew 38
Vizcaino, Alexander 97
Voit, Luke 40
Volpe, Anthony 76, 93
Wade, Tyler 76
Wells, Austin 77, 95
Yajure, Miguel 98

For the Joy of Keeping Score

THIRTY81 Project is an ongoing graphic design project focused on the ballparks of baseball. Since being established in 2013, scorecards have been a fundemental part of the effort. Each two-page card is uniquely ballpark-centric — there are 30 variants — and designed with both beginning and veteran scorekeepers in mind. Evolving over the years with suggestions from fans, broadcasters, and official scorers, the sheets are freely available to everyone as printable letter-size PDFs at the project webshop: www.THIRTY81Project.com

Download, Print, Score, Repeat ...

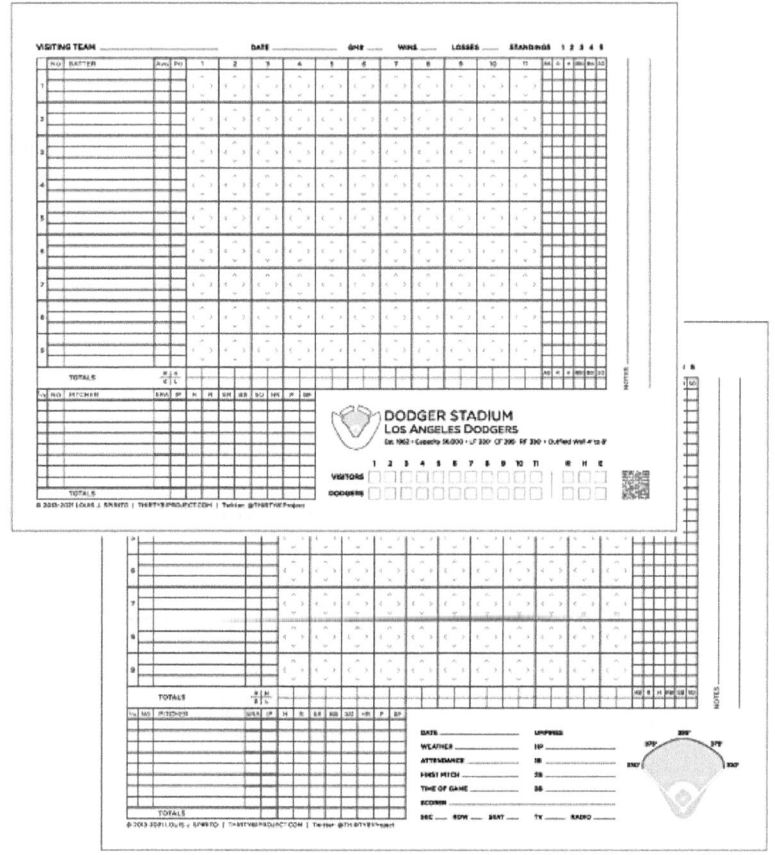

Scorecard design ©2013-2021 Louis J. Spirito | THIRTY81Project